THE PRICE GUIDE TO

TO

VICTORIAN FURNITURE

by John Andrews

published by

THE ANTIQUE COLLECTORS' CLUB
5 CHURCH STREET
WOODBRIDGE
SUFFOLK

Printed in England by
Baron Publishing, Woodbridge, Suffolk.

ACKNOWLEDGEMENTS

The author and publishers are indebted to the following, from whom many of the illustrations were obtained:-

John Phelps, of Messrs. Phelps & Co. of Twickenham, from whose extensive stock of Victorian and Edwardian furniture a wide variety of the photographs originate;

Sotheby's Belgravia, whose specialisation in the period has provided much valuable information;

Andrew Perry, of Wych Hill Antiques, Woking;

The Victoria and Albert Museum, whose Furniture Department were immensely co-operative, particularly with regard to the design books and catalogues mentioned elsewhere.

DESIGN BOOKS AND CATALOGUES

Extracts from the following design books and manufacturers' catalogues have been used as illustrations:—

Thomas King	*The Modern Style of Cabinet Work,* 1829 (1st Ed.)
Thomas King	*Cabinet Makers' Sketch Book,* 1835
Henry Whittaker	*The Cabinet Maker and Upholsterer's Treasury of Designs,* 1847
John Taylor	*The Upholsterer and Cabinet Maker's Assistant,* 1850
Henry Wood	*Cheval and Pole Screens,* c. 1850
J. Talbert	*Gothic Forms applied to Furniture,* 1867
Wyman	*Cabinet Makers' Pattern Book,* 1877
James Shoolbred	*Furniture Designs,* 1876
Henry Lawford	*Chair and Sofa Manufacturers' Book of Designs,* 1855
G. Maddox	1882
The Furniture Gazette	1884
Heal's Catalogue	1884
William Morris & Co.	Catalogue c. 1900
Norman & Stacey	Catalogue c. 1910

We are indebted to the Victoria and Albert Museum for permission to reproduce these items.

PREFACE–PRICE BASIS

After the publication of the *Price Guide to Antique Furniture* in 1969, and its subsequent enlargement and reprinting up to the present edition, it became clear that there was an enormous demand for a similar book covering the Victorian period. The increase in interest in the once-despised era of Victoria's reign - at least as far as furniture is concerned - began in the early 1960s, when huge quantities of Victorian furniture were available very cheaply.

A fairly rapid increase in interest, inflamed by journalistic promptings, caused violent rises and fluctuations in prices during the middle 1960s and even up to the time when the Antique Furniture Guide was published. The export sale of Victorian, and subsequently Edwardian, furniture grew rapidly and still continues. With the enormous variation in quality of Victorian pieces, from a high degree of craftsmanship down to the poorest East End junk, undiscerning purchasers were in a difficult situation.

The last two years however have seen a gradual evening out of most of the greater anomalies in price that existed before. The subduing of demand in late 1969 and 1970 caused a considerable re-appraisal of the values of 19th century furniture and thus has resulted in a more predictable and sensible range of prices becoming the accepted norm. It is now, therefore, possible to predict with reasonable accuracy the range of prices within which collectors should be able to obtain the pieces illustrated.

We have once again used as a basis the prices of the better provincial and suburban shops where good value for money can be obtained. It is not our purpose to cover the exceptional pieces dealt with by London West End specialists. In the Victorian period, wider and wilder designs of more exceptional exuberance than any preceding period were used. There is therefore likely to be on occasion an appeal to something extremely personal in the taste of the collector. Where this is the case, the top of the price range indicated is unlikely to deter the collector from exceeding it; we hope, however, that it will help to indicate the measure of the personal appeal.

SOME NOTES ON THE VICTORIAN PERIOD AND ITS STYLES

At the time of the Coronation of Queen Victoria in 1837 the neo-classical basis of furniture design which had dominated Regency styles in the 1820s had given way to "Grecian" influences. Thomas Hope and George Smith's books provided examples of these forms which were used by the furniture trade until the 1850s. This heavier and perhaps debased Regency style was not however the one which we associate most strongly with the early Victorian period; it was from about 1825 onwards that the French Rococo or Louis XV style was used.

Known wrongly as "Louis XIV" at the time, the French Rococo was used largely by the growing number of furniture manufacturers who catered for the increasing and prosperous middle class which was a feature of the population explosion in England in the 19th century. In a way, there grew a two-tier system of furniture design in this period. Serious designers published books with the idea of qualifying the vulgar exuberance of the mass producers and were followed by manufacturers of higher quality and ideals. Beneath or alongside them the furniture trade pumped out, using new techniques and materials, huge quantities of furniture on a scale which was impossible for the traditional furniture craftsman to emulate.

The French Rococo style was light and elegant and characterised by flowing curves and scrolls; naturalistic carving was used and the upholstery involved was also exuberantly curved.

However, there was also a liking for Gothic or Mediaeval furniture, exemplified by the Pugins, and for "Elizabethan" furniture, which was popularized through the influence of Sir Walter Scott's novels. Thus at the time of the 1851 Exhibition a wide variety of styles were in vogue and the confusion of the decoration of the exhibits is often held up to represent a low point in the history of English furniture design and manufacture.

By the time the International Exhibition of Paris in 1855 was held, however, the superiority of the French had had an influence. French designers were used by English firms and the Elizabethan style had declined as had the Grecian one. The 1862 Exhibition in London again was said to show an improvement, mainly due to the French influence. Lighter woods, such as walnut, satinwood and ash replaced the mahogany and oak of early Victorian furniture; the beginning of a revival in 18th century styles, which had hitherto been detested, began to show itself. By the 1867 Exhibition of Paris, the revival had become stronger, and many 18th century reproductions were made from this time up to the end of the century. Often these pieces were perfect copies, with the exception of the manufacturing methods used, and are now quite difficult to tell from the original Georgian items they reproduced.

In the 1860s the "Early English" or "Modern English Gothic" style became popular. It was used by William Morris, and is identifiable from its use of mediaeval-style joined woodwork with heavy pieces pegged together without glue. Talbert and Eastlake both propounded this style as well as Richard Charles. It was an extremely self-conscious style, using inlays and metal panels, but as a reaction from commercial production there was a demand for so-called Art Furniture which used decoration from spheres other than those of the furniture craftsman.

In the 1880s alliances of artists and designers with craftsmen produced the Guilds and Societies which made furniture to their high ideals. The first was the Century Guild, founded by an architect, A.H. Mackmurdo, who used Art Nouveau forms. Various other such Guilds and Societies eventually led to the formation of the Arts and Crafts Exhibition Society, which held exhibitions irregularly from 1888 to 1899. The English designers, including C.F.A. Voysey, and the Scotsman, C.R. Mackintosh, played important parts in the creation of European Art Nouveau.

The later Victorian period, however, also saw such styles as the Free Renaissance, based on 16th century Italian and French designs, the Quaint - a sort of arty-crafty Art Nouveau, and the Anglo-Japanese, sometimes using bamboo, all vying with each other. Taking these, together with the copies of Queen Anne, Chippendale, Sheraton, Adam and Hepplewhite, which were commercially popular, it is clear that at the end of the century the designers' battle for soundly-based originality was lost almost entirely.

A CHRONOLOGY OF THE 19th CENTURY

1 PERIODS

Year	Monarch	Period Appellation
1800–1811	George III	Late Georgian
1811–1820	George III	Regency
	- Prince George as Regent	
1820–1830	George IV	Regency
1830–1837	William IV	Late Regency or William IV
1837–1860 approx.	Victoria	Early Victorian
1860–1901	Victoria	Late Victorian
1901–1910	Edward VII	Edwardian

2 EVENTS

Year	Event
1807	Publication Thos. Hope *Household Furniture*
1808	Publication George Smith *Household Furniture*
1820	Publication A.C. Pugin *Gothic Furniture*
1825	Jennens & Bettridge obtain patent for decorating papier-mâché with pearl-shell inlay.
1826	Publication George Smith *Cabinet Maker & Upholsterer's Guide.*
1826	Publication P. Nicholson *Practical Carpentry, Joinery and Cabinet Making.*
1829	Publication T. King *The Modern Style of Cabinet Work*
1833	Publication J.C. Loudon *Encyclopedia of Cottage, Farm & Villa Architecture.*
1834	Coalbrookdale Iron Co. begin to make ornamental castings in iron.
1835	Publication A.W. Pugin *Gothic Furniture in the Style of the 15th Century.*
1836	Publication H. Shaw *Specimens of Ancient Furniture..*
1840	Publication H.W. & A.Arrowsmith *The House Decorator and Painter.*
1845-50	Thos. Jordan patents wood carving machine.
1847	Publication H. Whitaker *House Furnishing Decorating and Embellishing Assistant.*

1849	The Art Journal commences publication.
1851	The Great Exhibition, Crystal Palace, London.
1855	International Exhibition, Paris.
1860	Publication Richard Charles *Cabinet Makers' Monthly Journal of Designs.*
1861	Foundation of Morris, Marshall Faulkner & Co.
1862	International Exhibition, London.
1865	Morris Marshall Faulkner & Co. re-organised as Morris & Co.
1867	Paris Exhibition.
1867	Publication B. Talbert *Gothic Forms Applied to Furniture.*
1868	Publication Charles Lock Eastlake *Hints on Household Taste.*
1876	Publication B. Talbert *Examples of Ancient and Modern Furniture.*
1881	Publication R. Edis *The Decoration and Furniture of Town Houses.*
1882	The Century Guild founded by A.H. Mackmurdo and Selwyn Image - Art Nouveau designs used.
1888	Arts & Crafts Exhibition Society founded.
1890 et seq.,	C.F. Voysey first designs come out. C.R. Mackintosh designs. "Quaint" furniture commences. 18th century reproduction designs dominate commercial furniture.

HOW TO USE THIS GUIDE

The price ranges shown are an indication to private individuals of what should be obtainable. Where prices asked by dealers are substantially different no useful purpose is served by commenting on the fact. To maintain a particular standard or size of stock a dealer may be forced to purchase at higher prices than those envisaged at the time of publication because of vagaries in local supply and demand, particularly in the wake of an expert buyer. It is not the object of this publication to disparage individual dealer's prices.

The price brackets quoted are designed to cover the prices illustrated. The position of a piece can be further defined by the possession of "value points" sometimes shown. These are defined as follows:—

* A minor feature which influences prices to a degree affected by a number of other features, particularly of higher value.
** A feature of some importance in placing the piece within the price bracket, also affected by other features of higher value.
*** A feature which places the piece towards the top of the bracket.
**** A feature which lifts the piece over the top of the range, often by a significant amount.

Where possible the pieces are listed in chronological order, for convenience. The Victorian period was subject to a wide variety of styles, some of which were made over a long period. Style and taste could not be dictated, as in the 18th century, by a small group of rich men in London since the population had become too large and there was an ever-increasing middle class with its own requirements. We have tried to give a representative and sequential selection of the pieces more commonly available. We believe that this book will provide a useful complementary publication to the few standard text books on the subject, of which we would most strongly recommend the following:—

Victorian Furniture — R.W. Symonds and B.B. Whineray - Country Life.
Victorian Furniture — Simon Jervis - Ward Lock & Co.
The English Home — Doreen Yarwood - Batsford.

INDEX

PRICE REVISION LISTS

1st JANUARY

The usefullness of a book containing prices rapidly diminishes as market values change, for prices can fall as well as rise.

In order to keep the prices in this book fully up-dated a revised price list will be issued on January 1st each year. These lists will contain the current values of all the pieces illustrated in the book.

To ensure that you receive the Price Revision Lists yearly, complete a banker's order form and send it to the Antique Collectors' Club now.

Price revision lists cost £0.95p a year by banker's order, from:—

THE ANTIQUE COLLECTORS' CLUB
5 CHURCH STREET,
WOODBRIDGE, SUFFOLK

C100

A very interesting early Victorian chair showing mainly the desire for 17th century design in the caning and treatment of the back, but with uprights turned instead of in barley-sugar twist. The front legs, however, are plumb in the 19th century and the little added carving under the seat front rail has a scrolled leaf motif more reminscent of rococo. Probably made c. 1835-45, but could easily have been copied later in the century, and probably intended as a hall chair, although Loudon illustrated a similar one - No. 2016 - in 1833 and described it as a drawing-room chair.

Price Range: *Single*   *£10 – £15*   *Four*   *£50 – £70*
                  Pair   *£20 – £30*   *Six*   *£90 – £110*

1

C101

An interesting chair of c. 1830-40, nowadays sold as "Regency", but which was made on into the early Victorian period. The broad top rail of the back is carved with floral decoration, echoed in the centre rail. The turned front legs are also reeded and the seat is of the drop-in type.

Price Range:	Single	£10 – £15
	Pair	£25 – £30
	Four	£60 – £90
	Six	£130 – £160

C102

A typical early Victorian chair in mahogany, in which the Regency influence is still strong. The wide top rail is carved with leaf forms, which appear also in the centre rail. The turned front legs have been carved also, and the front seat rail is moulded. There is a drop-in seat c. 1830-40.

Price Range:	Single	£10 – £15
	Pair	£25 – £30
	Four	£60 – £90
	Six	£140 – £180

C103

Four drawing-room chairs from Thomas King's *Modern Style of Cabinet Work* published in 1829. Note the similarity of the top left hand chair to C102, with the exception of the upholstered back.

Price Range: *Top left to right, as C102*

             Bottom left, as C102

             Bottom right, Single £15 – £20   *Four £120 – £150*

                     Pair £40 – £60   *Six £250 – £350*

C104

An early Victorian dining chair of c. 1840 in oak. Again the seat construction and style owe something to the Regency period. The broad top rail on the back is typical of these early chairs, but the turned and carved front legs are more elegant than their more bulbous descendants of the next decade.

Price Range:	Single	£10 – £15
	Pair	£20 – £35
	Four	£50 – £80
	Six	£140 – £180

C105

An early Victorian dining armchair, or "carver" similar to the previous
example but with the addition of the large scrolled arms which in the
late Georgian or Regency period would have been treated more simply
to continue the line down the front legs. A solid, comfortable chair
of sturdy proportions.

Price Range: *Single   £25 – £35*
                 Pair   £60 – £90
                 Pair and four single £150 – £200

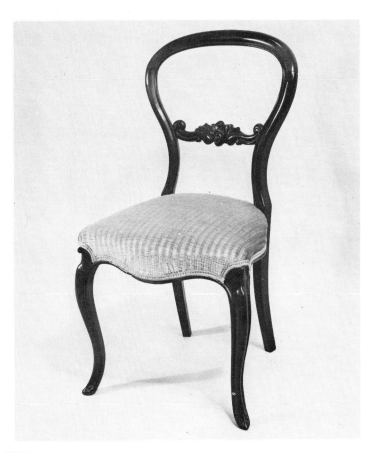

C106

A rather elegant balloon-back chair on cabriole legs with leaf carving on the centre rail. These chairs were intended mainly for drawing rooms and bedrooms even though made in sets. Perhaps our eating habits are now less robust, but these chairs have become enormously popular for modern dining room use. Made from the 1840s onwards in mahogany, walnut and rosewood.

Price Range:	Single	£15 – £20
	Pair	£30 – £45
	Four	£90 – £110
	Six	£220 – £260
Value Points:	Walnut **	
	Rosewood **	

C107

An early Victorian chair in mahogany with an upholstered seat. The balloon-back style is evident in an early form. This type of chair was made throughout the Victorian period, starting from about 1840. Note the hexagonal treatment of the front legs.

Price Range:		
	Single	*£10 – £12*
	Pair	*£20 – £25*
	Four	*£40 – £60*
	Six	*£110 – £140*

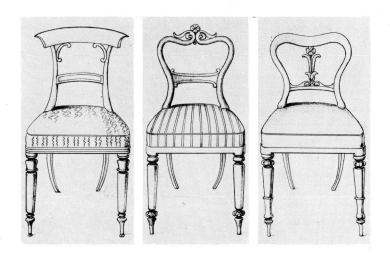

C108

Three drawing-room chairs illustrated in T. King's *Cabinet Maker's Sketch Book* of 1829. They clearly show the balloon back in its early form (centre and right) and the broad rail (left) of Regency models. Note the similarity in the turning of the front legs on all three chairs.

Price Range: *Left hand chair as C107 and C110*
                   Centre and right chair as C104

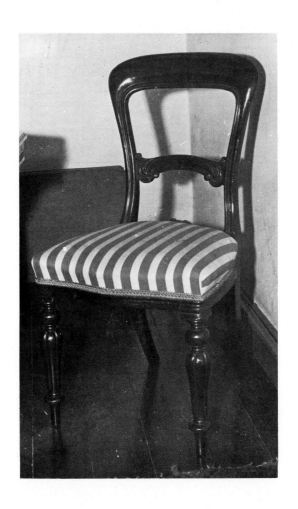

C109

A rather plain mahogany chair, probably of mid-Victorian period, with a hint of the balloon back but with a broad top rail described from late Regency influence. The turned front legs are also given a reeded treatment, leading to a plump, pumpkin-like effect. Almost certainly intended as a dining-room chair. 1850-60.

Price Range: *Single*   *£10 – £15*
                          Pair   *£20 – £30*
                          Four   *£50 – £70*
                          Six   *£100 – £120*

C110

An early version of the balloon-back chair, made of mahogany, with a drop-in seat construction following Regency practice. The turned front legs are also hexagonal in the centre section, leading to a rather stolid contrast with the more elegant back. Made from the 1840s onwards.

Price Range:
Single	*£10 – £15*	
Pair	*£20 – £30*	
Four	*£60 – £80*	
Six	*£120 – £180*	

C111

Another variation of the balloon-back, this time with a hefty construction but good quality carving in the back. The turned front legs are fluted in addition to having a carved top collar.

Price Range: *Single*   *£8 – £12*
                  Pair   *£18 – £25*
                  Four   *£40 – £60*
                  Six   *£90 – £110*

C112

Another derivation of the balloon-back in mahogany, with a broader and flatter top rail. The addition of leaf and scroll carved decoration gives a slightly heavy look to the top, but the cabriole legs are quite well formed. 1840s onwards.

Price Range:	*Single*	*£12 – £15*
	Pair	*£25 – £35*
	Four	*£70 – £90*
	Six	*£200 – £250*

C113

An elegant mid-Victorian drawing room chair derived from the balloon back, but with Gothic influence in the shaping of the back. The cabriole legs show a slight tendency to over-curvature of the knee but are nevertheless successfully blended with the overall style. c. 1845-50.

Price Range: Single   £15 – £20
                Pair   £35 – £50
                Four   £100 – £130
                Six   £220 – £260

Value Points: Walnut ***

C114

A chair similar to the previous example but less successful because the curves of the back have been combined with a straight section, leading to a little disharmony of line. Again derived from the balloon back with reasonable cabriole legs which nevertheless clash slightly with the squared back c. 1850. Note that the dot-dash grooving in the back appears in the furniture in Wyman's catalogue of 1877.

Price Range: *Single*   *£12 – £18*
                   Pair   *£30 – £40*
                   Four   *£80 – £100*
                   Six   *£200 – £250*

C115

A mid-Victorian upholstered single chair, probably made c. 1860 and showing the return to the French Louis XV 18th century styles which influenced the furniture trade at the time. It is made in mahogany and is fairly solid in appearance, although probably intended as a drawing room chair. Much reproduced.

Price Range: *Single*   *£18 – £20*
 Pair   *£40 – £60*
 Four   *£90 – £120*
 Six   *£230 – £280*

C116

A shield-back chair of clearly Hepplewhite inspiration but, in fact, made in the third quarter of the 19th century in solid satinwood. It illustrates how difficult it is now becoming to identify such Victorian reproductions from the original 18th century pieces, for such chairs in mahogany are very hard to date without dismantling them.

Price Range:	Mahogany	Single	£20 – £25
		Pair	£50 – £80
	Satinwood	Single	£25 – £30
		Pair	£60 – £80

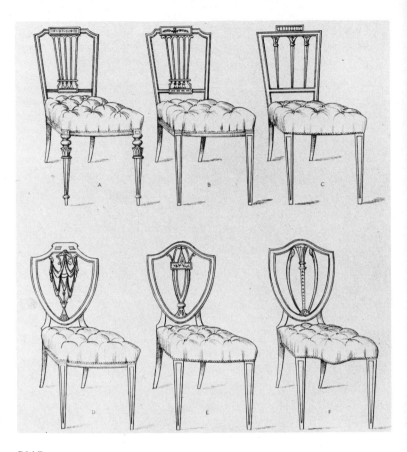

C117

A page from *The Cabinet Maker's Pattern Book* published by Wyman &
Sons in 1877 showing chairs in the ' Chippendale" style. This illustrates
the Victorians love of misnaming earlier styles since the chairs above are
in styles much more attributable to Sheraton, Adam and Hepplewhite.
However, it is likely that these 18th century designs were extremely well
copied and would now be hard to distinguish from the originals without
disassembly.

Price Range: *Top row   Singles £10 – £20 each*
                                  Sets of six or more £35 – £50 each
                  Bottom row (shield backs)
                                  Singles £20 – £30 each
                                  Sets of six or more £50 – £60 each

C118

A carved and painted arm chair of 1890-1900 period. The style is again influenced by 18th century designs and the front legs are scrolled and slightly curved.

Price Range: *Single*   *£20 – £25*
                   Pair   *£50 – £70*

C119

A late 19th or early 20th century mahogany chair in which again the styles of the late 18th century can be detected. The square tapering legs ending in a square pad foot are a little out of proportion with the slimmer moulded back uprights. A rather florid top back rail with scroll carving has been included to offset the severity of the rest of the chair.

Price Range:	Single	£5 – £10
	Pair	£10 – £20
	Four	£30 – £50
	Six	£60 – £80

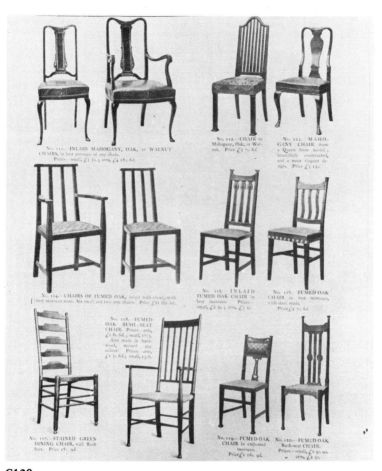

C120

A page from Norman & Stacey's c. 1910 catalogue showing chairs popular at the time. Points to note are that the top row shows Queen Anne styling, the middle row a slightly Morrisian influence, and the bottom row shows the country ladder back rush-seated chair of William Morris revival with two Art Nouveau chairs (bottom right), one of which is very similar to C119.

Price Range:		Single Chairs	Sets of six
	Top row	£10 – £15	£15 – £25
	Middle row	£10 – £15	£15 – £25
	Bottom row	£10 – £15	£15 – £25

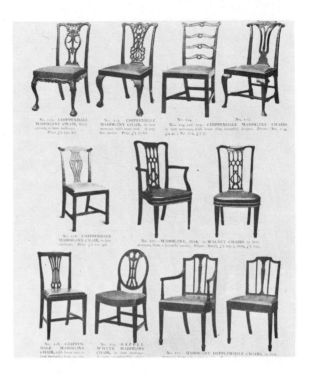

C121

Another page of Norman & Stacey's catalogue of 1904 showing outright reproduction of 18th century chairs. The proportions appear to be very good and at £3 or £4 each at the time these would have been high-quality chairs. Their dowelled construction and the lack of age provide chief evidence of their late origin but with suitable treatment and upholstery they can be made to appear to be very close to the real thing.

Price Range:			Single	Sets of six
Top row,	left		£20 – £25	£30 – £40
	left centre		£20 – £25	£30 – £40
	right centre		£15 – £25	£30 – £40
	right		£20 – £25	£30 – £40
Middle row,	left		£15 – £25	£25 – £40
	centre		£20 – £25	£30 – £40
	right		£15 – £25	£30 – £40
Bottom row,	left		£15 – £25	£25 – £40
	left centre		£25 – £30	£35 – £50
	right centre		£25 – £30	£30 – £40
	right		£20 – £25	£30 – £40

C122

Another armchair owing a good deal to 18th century Sheraton designs but almost certainly made after 1900. The Edwardian furniture makers seem to have found the addition of inlaid decoration in ivory and boxwood, to be seen on the top rail of the back, almost irresistible. Although the outward curve of the rather slim legs adds to the elegance of the chair, the turned upright arm supports are quite out of harmony with the square section of every other part of it. The maker has also been at a loss as to how to blend these uprights into the seat rail and has simply let them stop in mid-air, as in the case of many real Sheraton chairs.

Price Range: *Single armchair   £18 – £22*
                Pair armchairs   £40 – £50

C123

A late Victorian or even Edwardian chair showing the desire to get back to the 18th century in its design, which owes a good deal to Sheraton. The seat is of the drop-in type. There is much restraint in this chair, but the doubling-up of the top rail is something of a giveaway and the stringing lines on the square tapering legs tend to emphasise the slightly over-narrowed effect before the spade feet.

Price Range: *Single   £15 − £20*
                       Pair   £30 − £40
                       Pair with four single chairs £150 − £200

C124

A mid-Victorian hall chair of rock-like resistance to the posterior which was surely intended for ornament rather than use. The shield motif in the middle of the back is typical of this type of chair; it gives a hint of long ancestry and mediaeval lineage which are belied by the proportion and the front legs with their rigid turning. Note how the legs contrast with the softer scrolled forms on the back. The chair is mahogany, possibly c. 1840-50.

Price Range: *Single*   *£7 – £10*
                        Pair   *£20 – £30*

Note: J.C. Loudon, illustrating such chairs in his 1833 Encyclopaedia commented unfavourably on the decorated nature of the front legs compared with the back. The reason is, as he points out, that the front legs could be decorated by cheap turning work on a lathe, whereas the back would need expensive hand carving.

C125

Another mid-Victorian hall chair, featuring a more balloon-shaped back and the shield-like form in the centre of it. Again impossible to sit on for long, except as a penance. The legs this time have a double collar turning at the bottom, and stand rigid perhaps even more uncompromisingly than the previous example. Mahogany, c. 1850.

Price Range: *Single*   *£7 – £10*
              Pair   *£15 – £30*

C126

An interesting chair probably intended for use in the hall with an arcaded back, solid seat and heavy, much-turned front legs. It is a derivation of the "Early English" style propounded by Talbert and subsequently modified and lightened by Colcutt.

Price Range: *Single* £7 – £10
       Pair £15 – £25

C130

A papier-mâché chair, with inlaid pearl-shell decoration in a floral pattern and with a cane seat. Jennens & Bettridge obtained their patent for decorating papier-mâché with pearl-sheen inlay in 1825, but the chair, with its flowing cabriole legs and spoon-like back, probably dates from the 1840s. A wide variety of papier-mâché chairs were made, usually with cane seats and legs of the form shown in this example. The backs, however, followed the balloon, spoon, "Elizabethan", and other designs.

Price Range: *£110 – £140*

C131

A mid-Victorian papier-mâché occasional chair, the moulded back inlaid with mother of pearl and decorated flowers. Note the rather wavy cabriole legs, cane seat and the shape of the back, which owes something to the balloon back.

Price Range: *£110 – £140*

C135
A bentwood rocking chair with caned seat and back. Introduced to England by Michael Thoret, an Austrian, at the Great Exhibition of 1851 and made in large quantities throughout the last half of the 19th century. Some were ebonised. Many simpler forms of bentwood chairs and furniture still remain.
Price Range: £35 – £45

C136

A straightforward Bentwood café-style chair with pressed wooden seat. On the whole Bentwood chairs with cane seats are considered more desirable than the wooden ones.

Price Range: *£2 – £5 each*

C137

A selection of Bentwood chairs from *The Cabinet Maker's Pattern Book* published by Wyman in 1877. They show the versatility and elegance of which this furniture is capable.

Price Range: Single Chair   £2 – £5
                            Arm Chair   £8 – £15
                            Settee   £20 – £30
                            Rocking Chairs £25 – £40

PLATE 12

C138

A further selection of Bentwood furniture from Wyman's catalogue of 1877. Again the extraordinary versatility of this type of furniture is clearly illustrated.

Price Range:	Single chairs	£2 – £5
	Children's chairs	£15 – £25
	Tables	£25 – £45
	Rocking chairs	These are more elaborate than the examples in C135 and would be £30 – £50 each.

C140

A William Morris "Sussex" chair incorporating a traditional design with bamboo materials, emphasized in the painted decoration. These chairs were often stained green by the Morris firm - the well-known example in the Victoria Albert museum is similarly treated - and given simple painted decoration of this type. The caned seat does not look terribly inviting and the chair seems to be designed more for effect than for use. Chairs like these were produced by Sir Astley Cooper (1768-1841) and are thought to be correction chairs, designed to make children sit properly.

Price Range: *£30 − £40 each*

C141
A Welsh border oak high chair in original condition, probably dating from 1840-50. The reeded legs are constructed with the tenon right through the joint.
Price Range: *£40 – £70 each*

C142
A child's mahogany chair of c. 1860 constructed in a slightly unimaginative but robust fashion on the lines of grown-up furniture of the period. As with other childrens' chairs a bar could be fitted between the axis at the front in order to retain the sitter.
Price Range: £25 – £30

C143

A later Victorian high chair which can only be described, rather inappropriately, as deriving from the smoker's bow. It is made in beech and shows quite high quality turning on the spindles.

Price Range: *£15 − £25*

C144

A page from James Shoolbred's catalogue of 1876 showing three childrens' chairs in the centre. These would be made of beech, with cane seats and backs.

Note that two "Steamer" chairs are shown (bottom right), one with the foot rest extended and one without. These are again made of beech, with cane seats, and are very elegant when the wood is left natural and polished.

Price Range:	Children's chairs	£15 – £25
	Steamer chairs	£20 – £30
	Bedroom chairs	£10 – £20

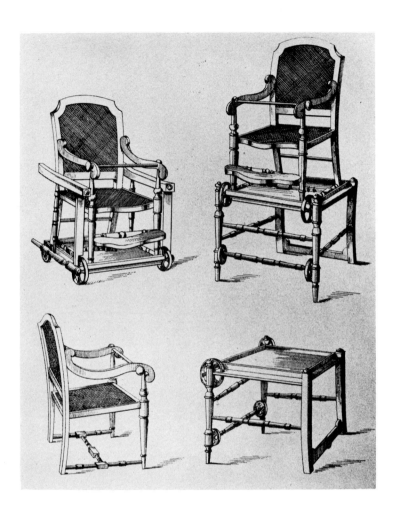

C145

An ingenious child's chair from Wyman's Pattern Book of 1877. As shown, the chair could be separated into a chair and table, or combined for use as a wheel chair or high chair.

Price Range: £20 – £40

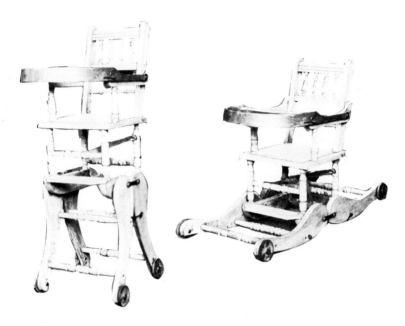

C146
Another ingenious child's chair shown in the high and low positions - a variety obtained by the use of finger-trapping catch mechanisms. The chair is made of beech, and is painted. Probably dating from 1880 or later.

Price Range: £20 – £30

C150
Described as a Garrick chair, this beechwood chair, simulated as bamboo, is painted green and white. Although simple, it is extremely elegant, the effect being heightened by the painting of the rush seat. Clearly stemming from Regency tastes, it could, however, have been made from 1830 onwards into the early Victorian era. The corner brackets between seat rails and legs are a delightful touch.
Price Range: £30 – £50

C151

19th century spindle back chair following the traditional Lancashire design, usually made in elm with birch or beech turned members, The pad feet on the front legs have been broken off. The genuine "Lancashire" version would probably have a rush seat rather than the solid wood one of this example.

Price Range: £15 – £25

C152

A ladder, or slat-back, country chair with a rush seat and shaped legs
ending upon buns. Often made in birch or elm and stained dark in colour. This example shows the way in which the country maker arrived at
a 'cabriole' form of front leg. Made from a much earlier period but also
through the 19th century in country districts.

Price Range:	*Single*	*£10 – £20*
	Pair	*£20 – £35*
	Four	*£50 – £70*
	Six	*£90 – £110*

C153

A typical kitchen armchair of the 19th century, on turned legs, much
beloved of schools and other institutions up to the present day. Usually
made in birch or beech and stained or varnished a dark colour. Sometimes the seat is made of elm. When stripped of stain or varnish to
their natural colour, these chairs are often a pleasant golden brown.

Price Range: Single armchair   £15 – £25
                Pair armchairs   £30 – £50
                Pair armchairs and four standard chairs: £70 – £90

C154

Another typical 19th century country chair, much used in kitchens but with a pleasantly arched and spindled decoration between the back rails. The chair is made of a pleasant golden-coloured beech, with an elm seat. Probably made in large numbers up to quite recent times.

Price Range: *Single*   *£10 – £15*
                        Pair   *£20 – £30*
                        Four   *£40 – £60*
                        Six   *£70 – £90*

C155
A late Victorian desk chair in oak, of the revolving kind. Until recently considered highly undesirable, but now finding a market, particularly since its modern equivalent became so expensive.
Price Range: *£10 – £20*

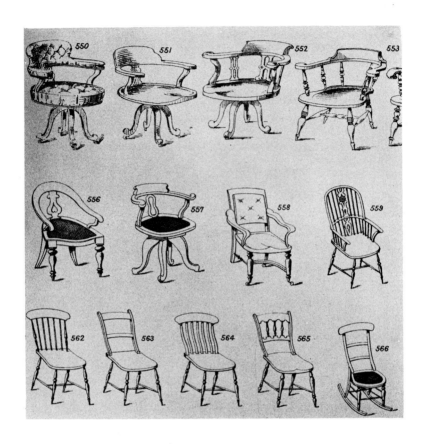

C156

A selection of revolving, smoking and kitchen chairs from Shoolbred's catalogue of 1867. Note their similarity to several of the other chairs illustrated in this section and to the Windsor chair, which remained popular throughout the period.

Price Range: *Top row*   *See C155 and C161*
                        Middle row   *See C155*
                        Bottom row *See C153 and C154 and C162*

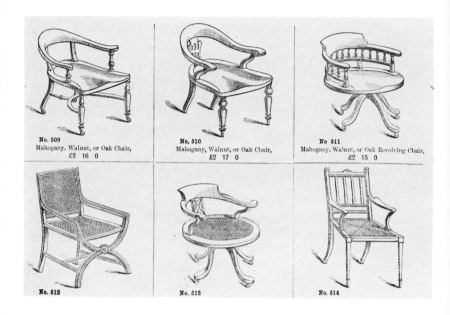

No. 509
Mahogany, Walnut, or Oak Chair,
£2 16 0

No. 510
Mahogany, Walnut, or Oak Chair,
£2 17 0

No 511
Mahogany, Walnut, or Oak Revolving Chair,
£2 15 0

No. 512

No. 513

No. 514

C157
A selection of smoking and revolving chairs from Heal's catalogue of 1884, where they were described as "dining room and library chairs". The two chairs in more classical style (bottom row, left and right) show how the return of 18th century influences had spread.

Price Range:	Top row	£10 – £20
	Bottom row	£10 – £30

C158

A bamboo rush-seated chair in which the influence of William Morris, the Arts and Crafts movement and the Japanese or "quaint" style are gaily intermingled. By the 1870s, leading firms were producing bamboo furniture cheaply to cater for the popular Japanese vogue. In this chair the traditions of Sussex and Tokyo have been determinedly blended.

Price Range: *Single*   *£5 – £10*
                      Sets   *£10 – £15*

C159

A turned armchair with a rush seat, very similar to those produced by the William Morris firm from 1865 onwards. Derived from traditional country chairs and much favoured by the Arts and Crafts movement, this type of chair was produced to the end of the century and beyond by firms catering for the "cottage" styles which designers like Robert Edis and E. Knight advocated.

Price Range: £15 – £25

C160

A 19th century Mendlesham chair, which the Antique Collectors' Club, being based at Woodbridge, is determined that the author shall feature prominently. Although elsewhere this chair would be taken as just another Kitcheny-Windsory chair with bobbles in the back, it brings tears to the eyes of East Anglians anywhere within 60 miles of Mendlesham. The names of the brothers Day, who originated this style at their native village in Suffolk, are normally bandied about heavily by cognoscenti of the species, and the author is assured that John rather than Dan made this chair because of some feature or another.

Price Range: £100 – £140 in East Anglia

Note: Yew is not normally found in these chairs, but other fruitwoods are common. Reproductions are now being made in Suffolk.

C161

The classic Smoker's Bow, a pleasant, well-turned and robust chair used in offices, public houses and kitchens during the later 19th century. The horizontal looped arms are made by screwing together sections cut by band saw. Mass production methods - turning and profile sawing from a template - were easily applied to this chair. It is no surprise to see it in Shoolbred's catalogue of 1867 - see C156 - but it is a surprise to see it in some West End stores currently priced at £27 or over. See below for the true value.

Price Range: £5 – £15

C162

A pleasant 19th century kitchen chair, very suitable for modern country kitchen use. Made in a light golden birch or beech with an elm or oak seat. The turning of the uprights and the arching under the broad top rail make this an attractive variety on the kitchen chair theme.

Price Range: *£3 – £5*

C163

Not all country chairs were made by simple country craftsmen. This oak armchair with rush seat was probably designed by R. Norman Shaw about 1876 and retailed by William Morris. It rests at the Victoria and Albert Museum who note that it was at the Tabard Inn, Bedford Park. The high back, with turned uprights and simple straight splat, owes a good deal to early 18th century chairs, but the turning on the front legs is much later in concept.

Price Range: £20 – £30

C164

A bobbin-turned yew chair with rush seat designed by Ernest Simson and of c. 1905 date. The bobbin-turning dates back to the 17th century and the style is derivative of that earlier period. Evidence again of the late 19th and early 20th century desire to get back to simpler and more natural styles.

Price Range: *£30 – £45*

C165

An oak armchair with rush seat, of about 1900 date, of English or Scottish origin. The Art Nouveau influence is very clear, particularly in the inlaid or stained black design in the centre of the back. The desire for restraint and simple woods in natural finishes is clear in this chair and C163 which represent the reaction from the over-ornamentation and vulgarity of much of the mass-produced furniture of the time.

Price Range: *Not usually found in shops. This is a special case, and is in the Victoria and Albert Museum. Nevertheless, similar chairs do appear from time to time, at about £30 – £50*

C170

A simple wheelback Windsor armchair of the 1830-70 period, but which has been made up to the present day, especially in single chair form. Usually the seat is made of elm, but the arms, back and spindles can be of yew - most desirable - birch, cherry, hickory, elm or beech.

Price Range:	Arm	£35 – £50
	Single	£20 – £30
Value Points:	Yew ****	

C171

A typical 19th century Windsor chair. The leg turning is in robust form,
echoed by the front arm spindles. The curved stretcher between the legs
- known as a Crinoline or "Caroline" stretcher - is often taken as evidence of 18th century origin, but this is not necessarily the case. It does,
however, add to value.

Price Range:	Yew wood	£70 – £90
	Otherwise	£50 – £70
Value Points:	Curved stretcher ***	

C172
A late 19th century chair which is a cross between a Windsor and a kitchen or office chair. It is very ornate, as the turning and the fretting of the centre splat show. There are still plenty of them about, although there has tended to be a drain of all these types of chair, particularly the Smoker's Bow, to the export trade.
Price Range: *£20 – £25*

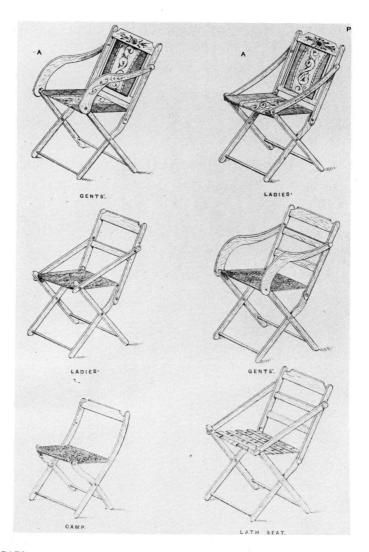

GENTS'.

LADIES'

LADIES'

GENTS'.

CAMP.

LATH SEAT.

C173

A selection of Victorian folding chairs from *The Cabinet Makers' Pattern Book* published by Wyman in 1877. For some reason the ladies never qualified for the convex thick arms of the gentlemen's versions. Now very much superseded by aluminium.

Price Range: £2 – £5

C200

A rosewood armchair of c. 1830, showing a high degree of craftsmanship. The front legs are heavily scrolled and end in paw feet. The arms are also scrolled and gilded. Even the back legs have been decorated with scrolled carving.

Price Range: *£100 – £150*

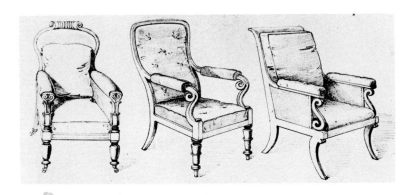

C201

Three chairs from T. King's *Cabinet Maker's Sketch Book* of 1829. Note that (right) the sabre leg was still evident. The chairs have not yet reach- ed the highly curved and scrolled "naturalistic" style, but are moving towards it.

Price Range: *Left*   £40 – £50
                   Centre   £40 – £55
                   Right   £50 – £70

C202

A deeply-buttoned leather armchair made about 1840. Although the chair is on turned legs the carving and scrolling of the arms is typical of the more exuberant approach of the early Victorian period.

Price Range: *Single*   *£80 – £100*
                        Pair   *£180 – £210*

C203

A buttoned low chair of the early Victorian/late Regency period made of mahogany. The curling of the arms is a development of the Regency style and the flowing 'X' form of the frame conveys considerable elegance.

Price Range: *£50 – £75*

C204

A classic armchair of the early Victorian period: elegant, well-proport-
ioned yet curvaceous, crisply carved and perfectly upholstered. The
cabriole legs, scrolling in the carving, and the open arms follow the influence of French styles, which was in its heyday in the 1850s. Only one
drawback; the joints at the rail/front legs and back/seat frame tend to
be weak structurally; not a chair to be too rumbustious upon.

Price Range: *£90 – £100*
                 With ladies' chair *** See C205.

C205

The "ladies' chair" companion to the previous example. The same excellence applies; crisp carving, smart proportion, deep buttoning, flourishing cabriole legs. A classic spoon-back that was popular and made throughout the period. Unfortunately, many versions were made much more cheaply and in woods much inferior to the mahogany of this example. Walnut and rosewood (rare) are in a similar quality bracket to mahogany, but beware the stained birch or beech of later examples.

Price Range: *£60 – £80*

C206

A small upholstered occasional chair with a back of shell, or serrated, shape. The mahogany legs are derived from the cabriole and show scrolling with "naturalistic" carving at the top. They are, however, rather straighter than a true cabriole and have lost a little of their elegance in the alteration.

Price Range: *£35 – £50*

C207

A mid-Victorian armchair which is button-backed. The shape is fairly typical of drawing-room chairs made in large numbers at the time, with scrolling on the arms and turned legs. The deep buttoning of the back would not have been extended to the seat in the original. 1840-50.

Price Range: £40 – £60

C208

A pair of mid-Victorian 'Louis XIV' chairs which in fact copy Louis XV styles. These 'half-age' or reproduction chairs are considered highly desirable since the style is a perennial favourite and is expensive to reproduce now. (Most modern reproductions of this type came from Italy or Spain).

Price Range: £100 – £140

C209

An upholstered armchair of the 1840–1870 period on cabriole legs of typical scrolled design. On many of these chairs the buttoning was also extended to the seat in the original design. This chair has been re-upholstered and covered in velvet but the buttoning is of nearly equal depth to the original.

Price Range: £50 – £70

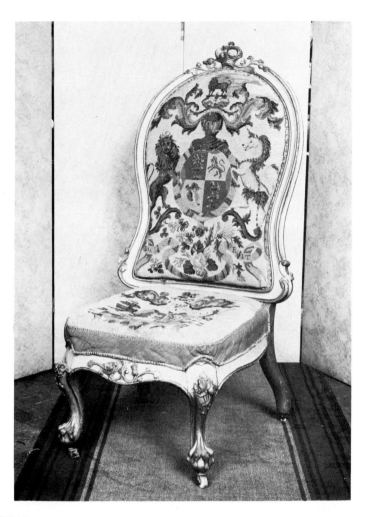

C210

A rather grand carved spoon-back chair with needlework upholstery. The cabriole legs and front rail show very clearly, in the decorative carved detail, the French influence known as "Louis XIV" and actually following Louis XV styles. The back is a spoon-back with crisply carved detail at the top. These chairs were made in huge quantities with all kinds of variety of shape, but not often with lion-paw carved feet, as in this example.

Price Range: £80 – £120

C211

A first-class example of a mixture of styles. The back of this mahogany
low chair is in what the Victorians called the "Elizabethan" manner,
with spiral-turned uprights – actually belonging to the Restoration
(1660) rather than the Elizabethan (1558–1603) period. The legs,
however, owe nothing to the style of the back and are typical early
Victorian cabrioles following the Louis XV or French Rococo (mis-
named Louis XIV by the Victorian) style then popular. Probably made
in the 1840s and, for all that, not an unpleasant chair.

Price Range: *£40 – £60*

C212
An extraordinary mahogany Victorian armchair, possibly intended for office or study use. The large seat is deeply buttoned and covered in leather. The back of the chair is similar to many dining chairs of the mid-Victorian period, but the arms, curving rather clumsily out to the scrolled uprights, give the chair a somewhat crab-like appearance. The cabriole front legs are extremely sturdy looking, rather than elegant, which adds to the impression of the chair being intended for a man in office or study.
Price Range: *£20 – £30*

C213

A typical small early Victorian drawing room chair in mahogany on cabriole legs. The chair appears to have suffered somewhat as regards upholstery and the buttons may have been added later. About 1845 in date; it can be seen that the castors have also been replaced at the front or back at some stage.

Price Range: *£30 – £50*

C214

A later Victorian (c.1870 onwards) buttoned chair with a balustrade
between seat and back. The style of the legs and uprights owes a lot to
the renewed influence of French furniture in the 1860s. The style is
compact, but elegant, and the fluting of the legs is an improvement
over the usual turning.

Price Range: £60 – £80

C215

An armchair of 1880-90 date with inlaid decoration of the type usually associated with "Edwardian Sheraton" furniture. The circular design of the chair is fairly typical of the Victorian period, and the front legs with their collars and fluted treatment also follow the turns that later 19th century manufacturers appear to have found irresistible. It is interesting to compare this with the more French design of the preceding example.

Price Range: £60 – £80

C216

A late Victorian smoking or study chair which exhibits the balustrade principle taken somewhat to excess. The effect would be considerably more attractive if the turning of spindles and legs were not so fussy and yet mean. A bolder, simpler form of turning would add considerable attraction — and value — to the chair.

Price Range: *£30 — £50*

C217

A bergère chair of the 1850s in Virginian walnut, with the same scroll carving and cabriole legs of French Rococo derivation that other chairs of the 1840s and 1850s exhibit. A loose cushion would have been fitted in the seat. Note how the back top rail — made from one piece of wood — curves boldly and rolls into a scroll at each end.

Price Range: *£80 – £110*
Value Points: *Decorative carving ***
                      Condition of caning *

C218

A rosewood bergère caned armchair owing something more to Regency styles than Victorian ones, but probably made from the 1830s or into the 1880s. In fact R.W. Edis's book on Town Houses, dated 1881, illustrates one (together with several other styles) in a drawing of a study. The curl of the arms and the turning of legs, however, are very Regency in feeling. The back top rail rolls over into a scroll at each end. The seat cushion is covered in leather.

Price Range: *£80 – £100*
Value Points: *Brass decoration **
                   Rosewood **

C219
A bergère or caned armchair of c.1875 with tulip chintz covering by
William Morris. This shape of chair, with either caned or fully uphol-
stered treatment, usually on square tapering legs, was extremely popular
up to 1914. See C229 for a 1910 example.
Price Range: *£40 – £60*

C220

A later Victorian — 1860-1870 — low chair, inlaid and decorated with burr woods on the back and raised on turned front legs. It is a natural descendant of the small spoon-back chairs of the 1840s and 1850s. This example has been re-upholstered in velvet, but the back upholstery could well have been buttoned originally also. Note the squareness of style associated with the later Victorian and the Edwardian period.

Price Range: *£40 — £60*

C221
Another low chair, on cabriole legs, with buttoned upholstery to the back. The shape is more flowing and "naturalistic" than the previous one, with back being an adaptation or version of the spoon back. Probably made in the 1850s.
Price Range: *£50 – £70*

C222
A typical mid-Victorian easy chair with balustraded support to the open arms. The back is fairly square in shape with a high curved top rail decoration by a semi-classical motif at the top. The leaf carving and scrolling of the arms is, however, similar to the curved designs of the earlier period.
Price Range: *£25 – £40*

C223

A typical armchair of the later Victorian period, possibly c. 1890. The design was used on into the Edwardian period, with the addition of suitable inlays, and this example, with its boxwood stringing lines and plain square back, could also have been made after the turn of the century. The wooden arms, with their upholstered top, and the turned balusters in a gallery all round the seat, were used on such chairs from the 1870s.

Price Range: *£25 – £40*

C224

A selection of chairs from Shoolbred's design book of 1876 showing
highly buttoned arm and low chairs. The styles are either those following the earlier period, as in the case of the low chairs, or simply
non-existent and rather lumpily functional in the case of the arm
chairs.

Price Range: *£50 – £75*

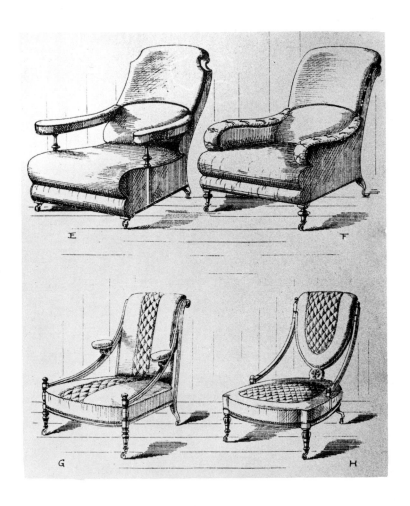

C225
Four chairs from Wyman's *Cabinet Makers' Pattern Book* of 1877
showing two rather half-hearted arm-chairs and two (bottom row) rather
French designs of which the right hand one, without the arm pads, is
the more successful.
Price Range: *£30 − £50*

C226

A rather extraordinary adjustable chair, on castors, which owes something to the Steamer chair in its design. The turned split-knob decoration, missing in one or two places, is a very Victorian feature of the design.

Price Range: *£30 – £50*

C227
A splendid Art Nouveau chair in mahogany with floral inlay, c. 1897.
The square tapering uprights with their flat tops, repeating the foot
design, are typical of this style and may be seen on other Art Nouveau
furniture. An excellent example of the updating of the saddle back
chair.
Price Range: *£75 — £100*

C228

An Art Nouveau corner chair which succeeds in looking both flimsy and yet rock-hard to sit on at the same time. Presumably intended more for ornament than use. Note, however, the square uprights ending in flat platforms, typical of the species. The inlay is of boxwood or ivory.

Price Range: *£10 – £20*

No. 290. LARGE CLUB EASY CHAIR, well upholstered and covered in best morocco, any shade. Price £11 11s.

No. 291. DIVAN EASY CHAIR in embossed morocco, any shade. Price £9 12s.

No. 292. EASY ARMCHAIR, with pillow-shaped back and seat, in best embossed morocco. Price £9 9s.

No. 293. LUXURIOUS EASY CHAIR, thoroughly well upholstered and covered in tapestry. Price £8 8s.

No. 294. EASY CHAIR of antique design, covered in tapestry. Price £6 10s.

No. 295. EASY CHAIR of an original design. Price £6 6s.

No. 296. EASY ARMCHAIR, in tapestry.

No. 297. EASY CHAIR, covered in tapestry, with loose cushion seat.

C229

Chairs from Norman & Stacey's catalogue of c.1910, showing a saddle-back (centre) and other 18th century designs.

Price Range: £40 – £70

C230
An armchair of 1890-1900 showing again the return to 18th century designs. In this case the legs show a Sheraton influence, particularly in the stringing and cross banding of the seat rail.
Price Range: £50 – £75

C231

Another armchair of c. 1900, with Sheraton influence in the square tapering legs and the satinwood inlaid shell motifs to be seen in the back uprights. The whole design shows a return to the late 18th century for inspiration.

Price Range: £20 – £35

C232
A papier-mâché armchair of c. 1845. It is something of an unusual
application, showing the well-known design of such chairs − cabriole
legs etc. − embellished with the mother-of-pearl and shell inlays inescap-
ably associated with papier-mâché.
Price Range: *£75 − £100*

C240

A low chair, with needlework covering, on scrolled feet. The shape is an adaptation of the more curved Rococo styles and the depth of the seat gives a rather tub-like effect. Large quantities of such chairs, not necessarily with Berlin wool-work upholstery, were made from about 1845 onwards.

Price Range: £40 – £60

C241

A low chair with strong "prie-dieu" influence in the shape of the back. The carvings shows a marked naturalistic turn with its leaf motifs, but the extremely ripe-looking turned and carved bulbous front legs, with thin aggressive white castors, cancel out any leanings to French slenderness. Nevertheless, a extremely well-made chair in mahogany with crisp carving.

Price Range: *£30 – £50*

C242

A typical "prie-dieu" chair of early or mid-Victorian period. Also known as a "kneeling" chair and used for devotions. The horizontal top is used to rest the arms on during prayers. The legs are fairly typical bulbous turned ones, but the covering is rather more decorative than many of the period which were somewhat sober in design or religious in inspiration.

Price Range: *£35 – £60*

C243

Left: An interesting low chair, with Gothic shaping to the back, on turned legs. These chairs were popular from the early Victorian period onwards and the Gothic influence of this one suggests a late c. 1850.

Price Range: *£30 – £50*

Right: The combination of Gothic carving and bulbous turning was not limited to low chairs. The dining chair illustrates both features in exuberance.

Price Range: *£15 – £20*
                  Sets   £25 – £30 each

C244
Three prie-dieu chairs with Berlin woodwork coverings from *Cheval &*
Pole Screens, Ottomans etc., by Henry Wood, published c.1850. All
three show the influence of the "Elizabethan" style, but particularly
the two outer chairs with their spiral-turned uprights and finials.
Price Range: £35 – £60

C245

Known variously as an X, Dante or Savanarola chair, this was intended to indulge a taste for the historic or antique. The Victorians appear to have had a taste for these rather theatrical chairs and there are still quite a few to be found, usually covered in threadbare velvet or scuffed leather with brass-studded edges. Their origins were in Tudor and Stuart courts as far as England is concerned.

Price Range: £40 – £60

MUSIC-STOOLS, FOOT-STOOLS, AND AN HOUR-GLASS SEAT.

C250
Music stools, foot stools and an "hour-glass seat" illustrated in T. King's *Cabinet Maker's Sketch Book* of 1829. In the top row the bases of the stools show the forms we attribute to the Regency period, with (left to right) tripod, flat base and baluster, and flat three-footed base with octagonal column forms.
Price Range: £25 – £40

C251

An interesting stool of ebonised mahogany with a needlework covering. The spirally turned legs and stretchers are an example of the "Elizabethan" craze of the 1840s.

Price Range: *£25 – £40*

C252

Adjustable mahogany piano stool with needlework upholstery covering. The turned legs are reeded and their slight outward curve at the foot suggests an early Victorian period, possibly c. 1840. Similar base designs and thread mechanisms are to be found on Regency chairs and stools.

Price Range: £25 − £40

C253

Stool, with deep-buttoned leather top (restored) and with the legs and top formed into a continuous curve clearly inspired by the "X" form. The turned stretchers in combination with this form suggest that the stool originally was made *en suite* with a chair of equivalent design in the early "deck-chair" form. Probably c. 1850.

Price Range: £30 – £50

C254
A good example of a piano stool on a tripod base, showing the scroll carving derived from French Rococo styles. Note how the rather bulbous centre pillar is given a rather fruity treatment in carving. c. 1850. The recovering has not given the depth of buttoning to be found in the original.
Price Range: *£25 – £40*

C255

Another adjustable piano stool, this time octagonal, re-covered in velvet. While the turned legs are also reeded, like the previous example, they are more chunky and have no outward curve; the thick turned collar at the bottom is uncompromisingly stolid. Also probably made in the 1840s.

Price Range: *£25 – £40*

C256

A fine quality square stool of the 1850s with crisp scroll carving on the legs which have plenty of flow in their curves. Contrast this with the example of C257 and note how, in addition to the leg form and curving, the centre column above is much better balanced and proportioned; the design flows instead of being checked by chopped-off changes in the line.

Price Range: *£40 – £60*

C257

Another stool, this time with upholstery which is probably original, showing the depth of buttoning. The tripod base is again typical, but the treatment of the legs is rather meaner in design, with less flourish and more lumpiness. The pumpkin-like treatment of the turned and reeded centre column is more generous.

Price Range: £25 – £40

C258
A mid-Victorian rosewood stool with a woolwork covering. The frame
shows a flowing scrolled 'X' form supports at each end with a baluster
turned stretcher between them.
Price Range: *£25 – £40*

C259
A Victorian 'Queen Anne' stool in walnut. This is a good reproduction
of an early 18th century piece, showing the cabriole leg with its refined
forms of shell motif and ball-and-claw foot.
Price Range: £30 – £50

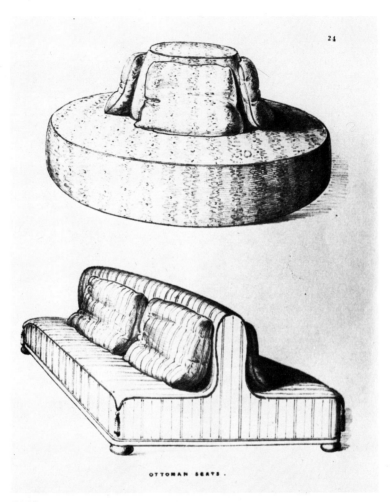

OTTOMAN SEATS.

C260

Two "ottoman sofas" from T. King's *Cabinet Maker's Sketch Book*, of 1829. The classical influence of the Regency period is very evident, particularly in the lower version. The shaping of the back is similar in both cases, but the upper example has clearly got a less elegant appearance due to the square, box-like appearance of the lower part. Neither design is a particularly popular one at present; the curly chaise-longue and the buttoned Chesterfield are very much more in fashion.

Price Range: Upper example   *£90 − £120*
      Lower example   *£100 − £130*

C261

A single-ended mahogany chaise-longue on turned legs with a high carved back showing same scrollwork in the carving. The bulbous turning to the legs appears harsh in comparison with the softer appearance produced by the curves of back and seat. Acanthus leaf carving appears on the back. It would probably have been button upholstered originally. 1840-50.

Price Range: *£50 – £70*

C262

A sofa from Henry Lawford's *Chair and Sofa Manufacturers' Book of Design* of 1855. Note that the classical design is still evident in the arms but the decoration has become much more "naturalistic" i.e. carved with leaf and other vegetarian motifs. The rather encrusted carving, with shield, at the back has made it slightly top-heavy and reduced the elegance of earlier and Regency examples.

Price Range: *£80 – £100*

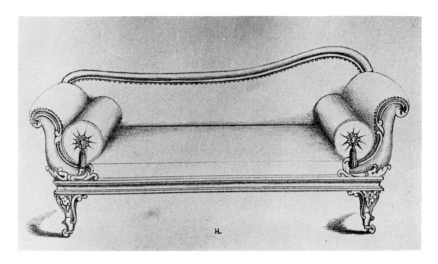

C263

Another sofa from Henry Lawford's design book of 1855. This one is much more in the classical style except for the cabriole treatment of the legs, with their scrolled carving. These given the later dating of the piece (1850-60) away almost immediately; with simpler or sabre treatment of the legs, this sofa could pass for Regency.

Price Range: *£80 – £100*

C264

An early Victorian mahogany chaise-longue of c. 1845-50 date. The design is relatively simple, but rather clumsy and unbalanced in that the high circular back gives the piece a top-heavy look. The turned legs have been fluted and there is acanthus leaf carving on the back.

Price Range: £60 – £80

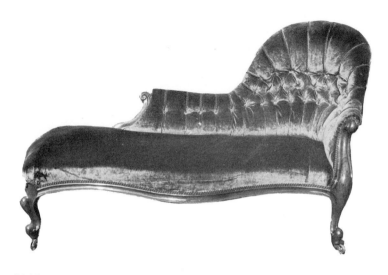

C265

A mid-Victorian single-ended chaise-longue in walnut. c. 1860. The button upholstery in the back gives a grand appearance and the scrolling of the legs is repeated on the arm and back. A highly decorative piece, probably part of a suite of drawing room chairs.

Price Range: *£120 – £180*
Value Points: *Walnut ***

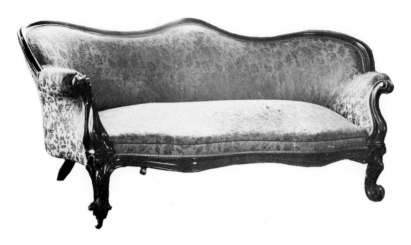

C266
A mahogany settee in need of upholstery, with carved and scrolled arms and front legs but fairly restrained undecorated curving to the back rail. The piece is more French in appearance than other examples and probably dates from 1855 - 1865.
Price Range: *£90 – £120*

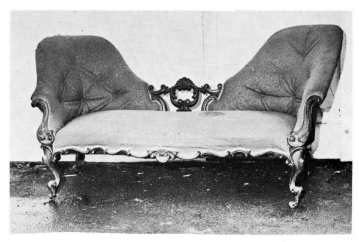

C267

A walnut settee in the "naturalistic" style or its derivatives, with florid scrolling which has involved a high degree of carving. The double ending tends to be more decorative than comfortable but the piece shows an exuberance and frivolity that is hard to resist.

Price Range: *£140 – £180*

C268

A fine quality settee in walnut, with the deep-buttoned upholstery in first class (probably almost new) condition. The piece is less frivolous than the previous example as far as wood carving is concerned, but is more elegant because some restraint has been shown. The back rail and the greater elegance, combined with the upholstery, make this a much more expensive piece.

Price Range: £270 – £300

C269

A sofa from Henry Lawford's Design book of 1855. This variation shows the centre panel, sometimes button upholstered, sometimes decorated with tapestry, that was used for those grander pieces. The legs and back exhibit much scrolled carving and leaf work, typical of the period.

Price Range: *£100 – £150*

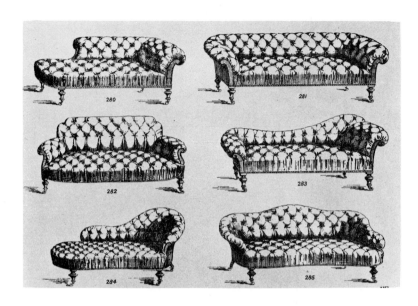

C270

A selection of buttoned sofas from Shoolbred's Design book of 1876. The examples cover the main varieties of the species. It is the Chesterfield sofa (top, right) which is the most popular at present and which is being mightily reproduced.

Price Range: Top row left   £70 – £90
                 Top row right   £180 – £250
                 Middle row left   £120 – £180
                 Middle row right   £70 – £90
                 Bottom row left   £70 – £90
                 Bottom row right   £110 – £170

Value Points: *If reupholstered in leather, at least 50% should be added to the above prices.*

C271

An ottoman centre seat and four other examples of sofas from Shoolbred's 1876 Design Book. The centre piece seems to have regained desirability as something of a curiosity (few modern rooms, surely, are big
enough to cater for them). All these fully upholstered pieces depend
enormously on the quality of their upholstery for their value.

Price Range:	*Sofas*	*£70 – £150*
	Ottoman centre seat	*£200 – £250*
Value Points:	*Leather **** (add 50%)*	

C272

A chaise-longue and drawing-room chairs from Wyman's Pattern Book of 1877. Note that the carving is rather feeble and clearly machine-produced. The religious tone of the top rail treatment doubtless contributed to the ponderous gloom of the Victorian drawing room.

Price Range:	Chaise Longue	£60 – £90
	Single chair	£10 – £15
	Armchair	£25 – £40

C273

An ebonised sofa of c. 1890 with an inlaid panel in the back. The piece is made in a style derivative of French and dimmer traditions, with a hint of the Prince of Wales's feathers thrown in this part of the suite of drawing room furniture. The overall effect is rather flimsy.

Price Range: *£60 – £90*

C274
Another late 19th century sofa in mahogany. The design of the back clearly derives from Hepplewhite styles, but the legs, which are of cabriole form, follow a later pattern. Again the effect is somewhat flimsy.
Price Range: £80 – £100

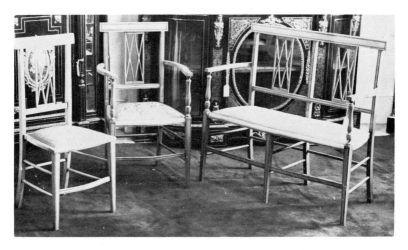

C275

A set of satinwood chairs and settee of late 19th century date, probably c. 1890. The originating design or at least its inspiration, is clearly Sheraton. The construction is, however, much flimsier, the result of an attempt towards greater refinement. Unfortunately Sheraton's own designs were rather effete themselves and it is difficult to imagine anyone over five stone in weight feeling safe on these even further weakened structures.

Price Range: *Set*   *£150 – £200*

C276
Somebody's version of Louis XV with fretted variations in the back.
Rather difficult to date, but probably late 19th century or even early
20th. The work in the suite is quite daunting but the effect is somewhat over-embellished. The chairs do have a generosity and flamboy-
ance which is appealing, though.

Price Range: *Suite*   *£300 – £400*

C277
A 19th century English reproduction of a French sofa, made with considerable skill and expertise. One of the great difficulties with the classic French designs from Louis XIV to Louis XVI is the fact that they have been so much reproduced and so accurately. Even now, Italian and Spanish workshops, as well as the French, are turning out Louis XV chairs on a grand production scale. The examples overleaf on C278 are a typical case.
Price Range: *£250 – £350*

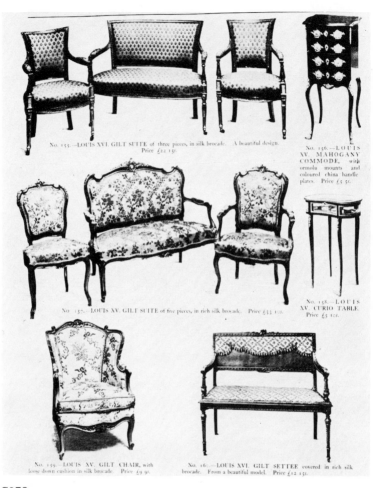

No. 155.—LOUIS XVI. GILT SUITE of three pieces, in silk brocade. A beautiful design. Price £22 15s.

No. 156.—LOUIS XV. MAHOGANY COMMODE, with ormolu mounts and coloured china handle plates. Price £5 5s.

No. 157.—LOUIS XV. GILT SUITE of five pieces, in rich silk brocade. Price £35 10s.

No. 158.—LOUIS XV. CURIO TABLE. Price £5 12s.

No. 159.—LOUIS XV. GILT CHAIR, with loose down cushion in silk brocade. Price £9 9s.

No. 16.—LOUIS XVI. GILT SETTEE covered in rich silk brocade. From a beautiful model. Price £12 15s.

C278

A page of reproduction French style sofas and chairs from Norman & Stacey's catalogue of c. 1910. How little difference there is in the centre row and the gilt wing chair from modern reproductions! And how many of these 70 year-old chairs may be presented as the real thing now?

Price Range:

Top row, Suite	*£200 – £300*
Top row, Commode	*£50 – £70*
Centre row, Suite	*£350 – £500*
Centre row, Curio table	*£60 – £80*
Bottom row, Chair	*£100 – £150*
Bottom row, Settee	*£90 – £120*

C279

A splendid page from Norman & Stacey's 1910 catalogue, illustrating vividly how the Chesterfield sofa has been a perennial favourite for 100 years. The two shown here (middle and bottom left) are most representative of the type. (Prices in 1910 were £6 – £10)

Very interesting is the Art Nouveau sofa (top right) with its typical uprights, where the front legs taper up to the platform echoing the fact. This feature is shown in C227.

The other settees show a simple comfort (top left) which is highly commendable and a rather less inviting 18th century derivative (middle right) which is less likely to attract nowadays. The box ottoman is a box ottoman: evening upholstery classes have lived off them for years.

Price Range: *Chesterfields*   *£120 – £180 (fabric)*
                                 £250 – £350 (leather)
               Settees   *£80 – £150*
               Ottoman   *£30 – £50*

T300

A walnut games and sewing table with chessboard top. The base, with its turned uprights and stretchers, is very similar to that of work tables illustrated by J.C. Loudon in 1833. The bag frame underneath appears to have been recovered.

Price Range: *£45 – £70*

T301

A rosewood work table of the early Victorian period, with a rather startlingly white work bag under the top. Note that the hexagonal centre column is very short and the top is supported on the hooped frame, which is cross banded with rosewood veneer.

Price Range: £50 – £80

T302

Another early Victorian work table with a folding top, a drawer and a silk work bag on a slide. The centre column support is very similar to that of the previous example but without the carved leaf decoration at the base. This example is in mahogany, which is considered less desirable than rosewood, but the folding top adds to value.

Price Range: £50 – £70

T303

An early Victorian work table with Pembroke-style flaps. There is a flat base supported on four feet and the hexagonal centre column is stepped at one third of its height. The dummy drawer fronts on the side illustrated are missing their handles or knobs.

Price Range: *£40 – £60*

T304

An early Victorian rosewood sewing box with a hexagonal top supported by a tapering frame, inside which the work box fits, suspended on its side. The flat base and column support are typical of the 1830-40 period.

Price Range: £40 – £60

T305

The later successor of the previous sewing table, showing the move to scrolled and curved designs in the base. Probably made between 1850-60 and onwards in large numbers. These tables are usually made of pine or deal, veneered thinly in walnut or mahogany. The octagonal top lid lifts to give access to a compartmented interior, and the tapering central column is hollow to allow for storage of materials.

Marquetry inlays were sometimes used to decorate the tops, which, being usually made of pine, often warp and therefore do not close properly.

Price Range: *Walnut   £40 – £60*
              Mahogany   £30 – £50

T306
A mahogany work table on scrolled side supports with a padded cross
stretcher on which the worker could rest her doubtless dainty feet. The
pleated silk bag may be original but the tasselled fringe has a somewhat
recent look. c. 1850.
Price Range: *£40 – £60*

T307
An inlaid work and games table on original white castors with rather fancily scrolled feet and side supports. The workmanship involved in inlaying the top, which is extremely decorative, should have merited a higher quality treatment of the base.
Price Range: *£40 – £60*

T308

An early Victorian work table in rosewood with ivory inlaid designs including a central harp. The hexagonal centre column and flat base follow similar late Regency designs which were made throughout the 1830 – 1840 decade and possibly a little later also. This example is clearly made to a high standard of workmanship and quality. We also show the same table closed, revealing the oval marquetry centre picture of a building and country scene.

Price Range: £130 – £180

T309
A work table of papier mâché inlaid with mother of pearl and ivory in floral and scrolled patterns. Note the basically flat base, with its four scrolled feet on castors, supporting a fairly simple centre column, following the designs of the late Regency period. 1850-60.
Price Range: *£120 – £150*

T310

A walnut work and games table with a folding top, the inside surface of which are inlaid with games boards. The work bag frame has been covered in velvet. The table is supported on double twist-turned columns with a similar stretcher between them.

Price Range: *£50 – £80*

T311

A Pembroke-type work table on scrolled supports, which are not as unusual as one might think. Apart from having a vaguely surprised look, as though it were about to glide away, the piece is a combination of a top in the style of the 1830s clapped on to a base in the "Rococo" style of the 1850s.

Price Range: *£30 – £50*

T312
An early Victorian work table in mahogany on a stretcher base. The squareness of the base pieces and their uprights contrast somewhat with the turned stretcher, but this appears to have been common practice in the 1830s and 40s.
Price Range: *£40 – £60*

T313
A rosewood work table of 1830-40 with a folding top and double
square column supports.
Price Range: £30 – £50

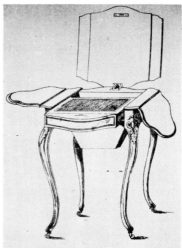

T314

Two designs for work tables from the *Furniture Gazette* of 1874. The example on the left is not far distant in design from those shown by Loudon in 1833 (see T300). The use of finials may be noted, however, and the Pembroke style flaps at each side.

The design on the right is, however, a result of the French influence on design and is altogether more elegant. T322 may be compared with this drawing to show the effect in practice.

Price Range: *Left*   *£50 – £70*
                       Right   *£90 – £130*
Value Points: *Walnut ****

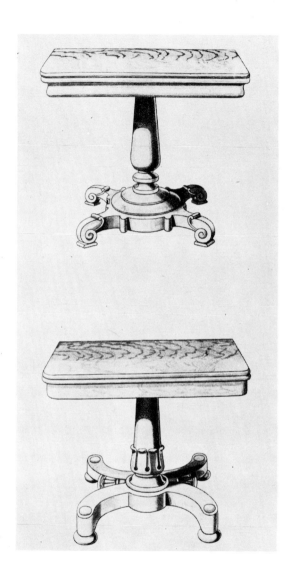

T320
Two card tables from the *Modern Style of Cabinet Work Exemplified* published in 1829. The styles are typical late Regency, but were still produced in the 1830s and the first few years of Victoria's reign. Clearly the top was intended to be veneered in figured mahogany, although rosewood was still in use.
Price Range: *£65 – £90*

T321

A simple mahogany card table of c. 1840. With this style of table the centre pedestal could be circular in section, as shown above, or hexagonal as with other tables. The top may be swivelled through 90° and opened, using the frame as a support. The inside is lined with baize.

Price Range: *£50 – £70*
Value Points: *Rosewood ***

             *Figured woods and inlays ****

T322
A walnut and mahogany games table, of fairly clearly French inspiration in design, although many were made in England. The slender legs have metal mounts, usually ormolu, and the top has a marquetry design inlaid in ebony and ivory. The inside surface is baize-lined, with walnut cross banding. 1850-60.
Price Range: £120 – £160

T323

A set of four papier-mâché tables of c. 1850. The tops are each differently treated, the largest having an inlaid and painted scene and the second inlaid as a games board.

Price Range: *£90 – £110*

T324

A folding side or card table in walnut, showing the four-pillar four-footed support arrangement used a great deal in the 1860s. The round centre to the base, with its turned finial, is also typical. Note the cabriole origins of the feet and their carving. The top turns through $90°$ to provide support when it is open.

Price Range: *£60 – £80*

T325

A combined games and work table. A chess board has been inlaid in the lid. The inside is divided into compartments into which working materials or games counters may be placed. The cabriole legs on the tripod base and the carving – rather stinted and machine executed – are typical of the 1850-60 period.

Price Range: £50 – £60
Value Points: *Walnut ***

T326

A folding card table in a typical late Victorian/early Edwardian adaptation of the "Sheraton" style. This example is made in mahogany and cross banded in satinwood with boxwood stringing lines down the legs. The X stretches with its upward curves and turned finial is inspired by even earlier styles than those of the 18th century. Much reproduced and popular in the 1920s and '30s. The handle on the drawer is a replacement.

Price Range: *£25 – £35*

T327

The card table of the previous photograph shown open. Note the top swivels through 90° to obtain its support when open.

Price Range: £25 – £35

T328
Another later Victorian/Edwardian mahogany games table, this time
with its original handles. The top swivels through 90° and folds open,
obtaining its support from the top underframe. Note the tapering legs
with stringing lines and satinwood cross-banding in emulation of late
18th century "Sheraton" styles. These tables were reproduced after the
1914-18 war.
Price Range: £25 − £35

T330

A fine quality early Victorian yew-wood circular dining table. The flat platform base with its three elaborately carved paw feet is a straight-forward continuation of late Regency and William IV designs. The system of veneering the top in triangular sections radiating out from the centre is one used for "feather" mahogany and other decorative woods to get the maximum decorative effect.

Price Range: *Yew*   *£140 – £180*
Mahogany *£100 – £150*
Rosewood *£120 – £160*

T331
A mahogany table made with figured veneers, possibly intended for drawing room use, but nowadays bought for use as a dining table. The base is rather heavy, with an extended centre column to cope with the depth of the scrolled feet.

Price Range: £90 – £120
Value Points: Walnut ***

T332

A walnut loo table of the 1855-65 period, with an oval-shaped top. It is supported on a four-pillar base on scrolled feet with a centre base decoration ending in a finial. The top is decorated with matching walnut burr veneers. Mahogany examples were also made but the walnut ones are more popular.

Price Range: *£100 – £140*
Value Points: *Walnut ****

T333

Another walnut loo table with an oval top shown in the tipped up position. The beautiful matching of the burr veneers is achieved by using four identical sheets and "quartering" the top as in early 18th century practice. The inlaid centre decoration and decorative banding are made from boxwood and ivory. A very decorative and high quality table, which could have been bought for about £10 some ten years ago. Old cabinet makers frequently relate how, as apprentices in the '20s, one of their first jobs was to divide the tops of such tables in half lengthways to provide two single bed-heads. The bases were split up to feed the workshop stove in cold weather.

Price Range: *£120 – £150*

T334
A walnut dining table of c. 1860 on which the four-pillar base has been developed into four sweeping scrolled supports to the top, plus the four scrolled and carved feet ending in leaf decoration. The top is shaped and quartered in matching veneers of a highly burred and decorative nature. Note the large circular centre at the base and its turned knob embellishments.
Price Range: £180 – £250

T335

A page of dining room furniture from Wyman's Design book of 1877. The table is robust, with bulbous turned legs, and of a type which follows the large extending tables of the Regency period. Indeed, many dining tables of the Victorian period, from 1840 onwards, must have followed a basically simple pattern such as this. The other furniture is not particularly attractive, but at least the chairs are upholstered for comfort.

Price Range: *Table only £15 – £25*

T336
Two reproductions of Tudor oak tables from William Morris's catalogue
of c. 1900. Both were described as "hall (or dining room) tables of old
English ship oak". Clearly the hall space must have been extensive to
cope with tables of this size, particularly if they were placed centrally.
Price Range: £35 – £50

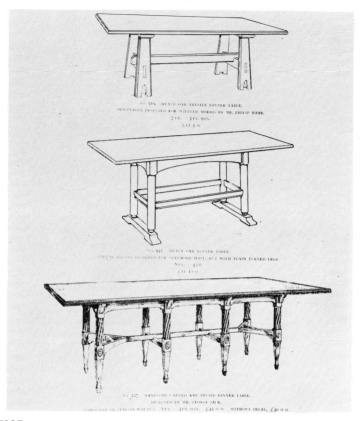

No. 318. HEAVY OAK TRESTLE DINNER TABLE.
ORIGINALLY DESIGNED FOR WILLIAM MORRIS BY MR. PHILIP WEBB.
7 FT. 3 FT. 9 IN.
£12 5 0

No. 511. HEAVY OAK DINNER TABLE.
SIMILAR TO ONE DESIGNED FOR STANMORE HALL, BUT WITH PLAIN TURNED LEGS.
8 FT. 4 FT.
£11 10 0

No. 337. HANDSOME CARVED AND INLAID DINNER TABLE.
DESIGNED BY MR. GEORGE JACK.
MAHOGANY OR ITALIAN WALNUT. 8 FT. 3 FT. 9 IN. £45 0 0. WITHOUT INLAY, £30 0 0.

T337

Three dining tables, again from the William Morris firm's catalogue of c. 1900. In these the design shows the contemporary desire to return to simple mediaeval forms, but without outright reproduction. The use of tenoned and pegged joints as both structural and decorative features and the desire to use trestles and central ties were all considered a welcome reversion from the mass-production methods of other late 19th century furniture construction.

The lower example was clearly a much higher priced item since it was carved and inlaid to a design by a Mr. George Jack. Whereas the top two pieces retailed at about £12, the lower table was £45 if inlaid, or £30 without inlay, and was made in mahogany or Italian walnut. The top table was 7ft., long, the centre and lower examples were both 8ft.

Price Range: *top and centre*   *£35 – £50*
                         bottom   *£100 – £150*

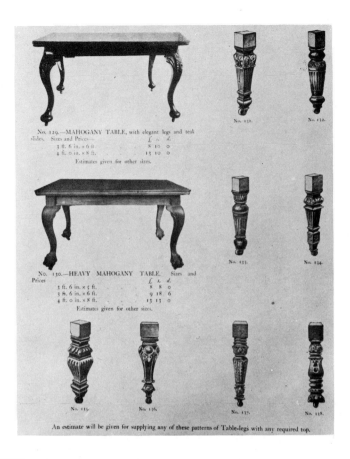

No. 129.—MAHOGANY TABLE, with elegant legs and teak
slides. Sizes and Prices—
            £ s. d.
 3 ft. 6 in. × 6 ft.   8 10 0
 4 ft. 0 in. × 8 ft.   13 10 0
   Estimates given for other sizes.

No. 130.—HEAVY MAHOGANY TABLE. Sizes and
Prices—
            £ s. d.
 3 ft. 6 in. × 5 ft.   8 8 0
 3 ft. 6 in. × 6 ft.   9 18 6
 4 ft. 0 in. × 8 ft.   13 13 0
   Estimates given for other sizes.

An estimate will be given for supplying any of these patterns of Table-legs with any required top.

T338

Typical heavy mahogany dining tables from Norman & Stacey's catalogue of c. 1910. They could be supplied with cabriole legs as shown, or with turned and carved legs to the examples shown on the same page. From being considered highly undesirable for the last twenty or thirty years, they are now being recognisable as extremely solid and useful working tables which could not be reproduced now without considerable expense.

Price Range: *£15 – £20*

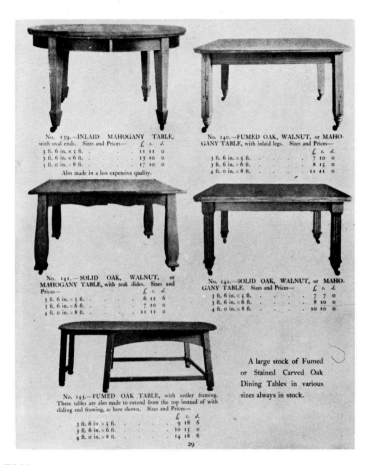

No. 139.—INLAID MAHOGANY TABLE, with oval ends. Sizes and Prices—

	£	s.	d.
3 ft. 6 in. × 5 ft.	11	11	0
3 ft. 6 in. × 6 ft.	13	10	0
4 ft. 0 in. × 8 ft.	17	10	0

Also made in a less expensive quality.

No. 140.—FUMED OAK, WALNUT, or MAHOGANY TABLE, with inlaid legs. Sizes and Prices—

	£	s.	d.
3 ft. 6 in. × 5 ft.	7	10	0
3 ft. 6 in. × 6 ft.	8	15	0
4 ft. 0 in. × 8 ft.	11	11	0

No. 141.—SOLID OAK, WALNUT, or MAHOGANY TABLE, with teak slides. Sizes and Prices—

	£	s.	d.
3 ft. 6 in. × 5 ft.	6	12	6
3 ft. 6 in. × 6 ft.	7	10	0
4 ft. 0 in. × 8 ft.	11	11	0

No. 142.—SOLID OAK, WALNUT, or MAHOGANY TABLE. Sizes and Prices—

	£	s.	d.
3 ft. 6 in. × 5 ft.	7	7	0
3 ft. 6 in. × 6 ft.	8	10	0
4 ft. 0 in. × 8 ft.	10	10	0

No. 143.—FUMED OAK TABLE, with under framing. These tables are also made to extend from the top instead of with sliding end framing, as here shown. Sizes and Prices—

	£	s.	d.
3 ft. 6 in. × 5 ft.	9	18	6
3 ft. 6 in. × 6 ft.	10	15	0
4 ft. 0 in. × 8 ft.	14	18	6

A large stock of Fumed or Stained Carved Oak Dining Tables in various sizes always in stock.

29

T339

A further selection of dining tables from Norman & Stacey's catalogue of c. 1910. The Art Nouveau influence has clearly permeated the commercial world here (centre, left) and oak, fumed or natural, was offered as well as mahogany or walnut in several cases.

Price Range: *£10 – £20*

T340

Three "fancy" tables from T. King's *Modern Style of Cabinet Work* of 1829. That on the left is clearly a chess or games table, while the others are circular tripod base types.

Price Range:	Games table	£25 – £40
	Tripod tables	£12 – £25
Value Points:	Walnut ***	
	Rosewood **	

T341

A mahogany ex-tripod table of early Victorian, c. 1840, period in which some Regency influence is still lingering in the hexagonal column but a faint hint of Gothic has crept in to the column base design. The original concept of a tripod of three legs has developed into a flat base on turned feet. The top is veneered in pine but the base is solid.

Price Range: *£15 – £20*

T342
An ebonised mid-Victorian "tripod" table with a much-turned centre column and again a flat base on turned feet.
Price Range: *£12 – £20*

T343

A square topped Japanned table on a turned column with tripod base, c. 1840. This form of decoration has a steady, if unspectacular, market and if the colours used for floral decoration are varied the pieces are extremely pleasant.

Price Range: *£60 – £90*

T344
The painted circular table of c. 1850 on a baluster turned column and circular flat base. The column and base are black lacquered and decorated with gilt painted floral scroll motifs.
Price Range: £120 – £140

T345
An early Victorian mahogany reading table c. 1835-40 on a plain
centre column supported on a flat platform base on bun feet. The 'off-
centre' nature of the table enables it to be used when the reader is
sitting on a chair or even in bed.
Price Range: £35 – £50

NB   See also B549

T346

A walnut drop-leaf gate-leg table of a type known in the trade as a
Sutherland table (for some obscure reason). Made in mahogany or walnut (i.e. veneered in figured or burr walnut) these tables can be supported on a single turned column at each end, as shown above, or on a
double column with spiral or other turning. There is an extra, thin,
turned leg on a gate at each side which swings out to support the flap
when open. They can be seen clearly above. The Victorians do not seem
to have minded this rather unhappy lack of cohesion in leg design; the
gate legs often look like a pair of poles or walking sticks that someone has
leant in random fashion against the frame under the flaps. The merit of
the design is, of course, that the table, when folded, is very slim in end
elevation and the whole is mounted on castors so that it can be tucked
away neatly. The spiral grooving turned into the legs of the above
example is often found on these tables.

Price Range: *Mahogany*   *£20 – £30*
                    Walnut, figured   *£25 – £35*
                    Walnut, burr   *£30 – £40*

T347
Another Sutherland table, this time with squared flaps and made of
mahogany. The end supports are spiral turned and the plain feet are not
scrolled. There is a typical 'thumb-nail' moulding running around the
top edge of the table. c. 1860.
Price Range: £20 – £30

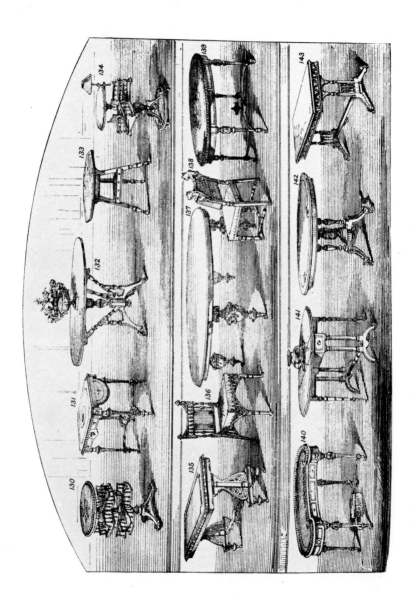

T348

T348

An interesting selection of drawing room tables from Shoolbred's catalogue of 1876.

Top row, far left and far right. Tripod occasional tables with balustered platforms radiating from the centre column. Usually in mahogany.

Price Range: *£20 – £30*

Top row, left centre. A table in the French Louis XVI style with end flaps. This type was often ebonised and inlaid with brass, with metal mounts.

Price Range: *£80 – £120*

Top row, centre. An odd circular table, not dissimilar to one shown in T327, by William Morris.

Price Range: *£20 – £35*

Top row, right centre. An octagonal table.

Price Range: *£10 – £20*

Middle row, left. A carved and decorated stretcher table, probably inlaid but mainly machine worked as far as carving and end fretting is concerned.

Price Range: *£30 – £50*

Middle row, centre. A large circular table on highly carved bulbous legs. Would now be used as a dining table.

Price Range: *£80 – £100*

Middle row, right. An oval table again in French styling, probably inlaid and decorated with metal mounts.

Price Range: *£150 – £250*

Bottom row, left. A kidney-shaped writing table with a brass gallery leather top and carved and fluted legs.

Price Range: *£100 – £160*

Bottom row, left centre. A Sutherland table.

Price Range: *£40 – £60*

Bottom row, right centre. A walnut loo table on a four-column base.

Price Range: *£80 – £120*

Bottom row, right. A stretcher table with machine carved frieze, the ends showing turned baluster decoration.

Price Range: *£60 – £90*

T349

A highly embellished Buhl (or Boulle) table of mid-19th century date now highly sought after by the Italian export trade. André Charles Boulle was a French artist of the Louis XIV period and the original marquetry of shell and metal which takes his name influenced designs in England. It appears to have had considerable popularity. This example exhibits a cartouche shaped top, cupid ormolu mounts, cabriole legs and scrolled stretchers centering in an ormolu urn.

Price Range: *£650 – £900*

T350

A marquetry centre table or library table of the 1850-70 period, with fluted column legs on brass castors. The treatment of the top is fairly lavish and the gadrooned edge is either gilded or of brass stamping.

Price Range: *£250 – £350*

T351

An oak table of c. 1880, octagonal in shape with turned legs. Presumably for occasional or library use and again an example of the desire for simpler furniture in undecorated woods following much earlier period styles.

Price Range: *£50 – £80*

T352
A rosewood corner table of 1900 - 1910 period, inlaid with boxwood and ivory. The square tapering legs are typical of the period and the prevalence of late 18th century styles for inspiration in design.
Price Range: *£15 – £25*

T353

Four occasional tables from William Morris's catalogue of c. 1900. The table on the lower right of the plate was available as shown or as a card table with a folding top. The tables were described as drawing room pieces and were clearly for occasional use. The influence of the 17th century is evident in the three straight-legged examples but the cabriole-legged version is clearly derived from the designs popular in the first quarter of the 18th century, so much so that it is almost a reproduction and was described as Queen Anne.

Price Range:	Top left	*£15 – £25*
	Top right	*£15 – £25*
	Bottom left	*£15 – £25*
	Bottom right	*£25 – £35*

T354

Four more occasional tables from William Morris's catalogue of c. 1900. Again, the designs are derived from the 17th and 18th century. The tables were available in fumed oak or mahogany. Again, that at the top right of the plate was described as Queen Anne (with glass for mounting embroidery) whereas the remainder were merely occasional tables.

Price Range:	Top left	£15 – £20
	Top right	£25 – £35
	Bottom left	£20 – £30
	Bottom right	£20 – £30

T355

A circular Tunbridge Ware tip-up table on a tripod base. A marquetry man's nightmare or challenge, whichever way you prefer it. Tunbridge Ware is made of the ends of hundreds of little sticks of woods, glued together in a pattern and cut across the grain to provide little sheets of veneer. From these a pattern was built up. Other items, such as workboxes and tea-caddies were made of it. c. 1870.

Price Range: *£90 – £120*

CHESTS

Lovers of 18th century furniture might claim that the Victorians' sole contribution to chest production consisted of wooden knobs. Certainly they were prolific vandalisers of 18th century chests of drawers, drilling large holes in the drawer fronts so as to insert the wooden spigots of the knobs they so preferred to brass scutcheons and drop handles. They did, however, make large quantities of chests of drawers, but they were not nearly as attractive as their 18th century counterparts.

What seems to have happened is that the chest of drawers became relegated firmly to the bedroom and was no longer required to decorate the rooms used in daylight. Other forms of storage space were used in drawing and dining room — chiffoniers, tables, sideboards, cupboards and pier cabinets. The chest of drawers was mainly used for clothes storage in the bedroom and, as such, needed to be large, commodious and utilitarian. Only later in the 19th century does much thought appear to have been given to its design.

It is true, however, that some attractive woods and veneers were used, particularly "feathered" mahogany and even satinwood. Design on the whole was square or bow-fronted, and the chests were often higher and wider than their predecessors. Many were made in cheaper woods and heavily stained and varnished to resemble mahogany. The present stripped-pine industry would have been bankrupt without them.

CH400

Possibly the epitome of the good quality Victorian mahogany chest of drawers — tall, bow fronted, with splendid use of "feather" mahogany veneers. Capacious, well-built and with drawers fitted to run smoothly. The wooden knobs have been turned with some decorative ridging which refines the bluntness of the ordinary bulbous knob. The bun-shaped and tapered turned feet are also typical.

The gradation of the drawer depths is also well handled on this example. Altogether a very professional piece of furniture but, unlike 18th century chests, not very suitable for rooms other than the bedroom and therefore restricted in price accordingly.

Price Range: *£35 – £50*

CH401

A smaller, shorter and blunt Victorian chest of drawers on rather interesting triple-bun type turned feet. The drawers are deep and give the impression that the chest was designed with some sort of top structure originally. Perhaps it was intended for use with a dressing mirror. In this case the wooden knobs are ebonised and quite uncompromising.

Price Range: £15 – £25

CH402

A military chest on turned feet. These chests were used by army officers up to the 1870's. The flush-fitting drawer handles and brass-reinforced corners are their characteristic features, as are the carrying handles to each half. Usually made in mahogany, but padouk, cedar and camphor-wood examples are found. Now much reproduced in a variety of woods, including "distressed" yew veneers and available in large quantities in reproduced form. There is not a lot of difference in price between reproductions and 19th century examples.

Price Range: £110 – £130
Value Points: *Rare exterior woods and drawer linings ***

CH403

A mahogany military chest of c. 1845, fitted with a secretaire drawer. This secretaire arrangement can be extended for the whole drawer length or confined to a smaller central section as shown above.

Price Range: *£130 – £170*

Value Points: *Style of secretaire fittings. (Secret drawers add to value, so does the number of small drawers and pigeon holes) ****

                 Rare woods and drawer linings ***

CH404

A typical Victorian mahogany chest of drawers of smaller size. The base design incorporates the flat apron to be found on so much Victorian furniture. The choice of the feathered mahogany veneers helps to lighten the appearance.

Price Range: *£15–£30*

CH405

A so-called 'Wellington' chest or more correctly, specimen cabinet, of c. 1850. It is possibly due to the fact that the hinged side pieces or flaps lock over the drawers to prevent their opening during carriage and hence a possibly military or compaign advantage that the Wellington sobriquet has been given. Perhaps the largest concentration of drawers per foot super, obtainable in any piece of furniture is achieved by these chests, which are ideal for numismatists or specimen collectors. The taller types were often used for cutlery. Velvet lined drawers often indicate that the original purpose was in fact for collecting and some examples have grooved glass lids to the drawers. The above example is made of mahogany but oak, walnut, rosewood and maple were used.

Price Range: £30 – £60
Value Points: Decorative veneers ***
                  Specially fitted drawers ***
                  (Glass lids, compartments etc.)

CH406

Two designs for chests of drawers in the (top) "Elizabethan" and (below) "Italian" styles, from Wittaker's *Cabinet Maker and Upholsterer's Treasury of Designs* published in 1847. Both designs show a 4ft., width for the chests, and both used wooden drawer knobs. Such designs did actually reach manufacture, although they are not found very commonly nowadays.

Price Range: *£25 – £40*

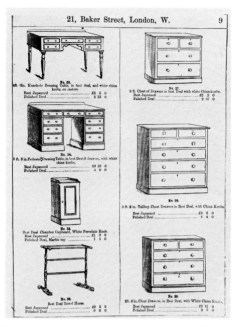

CH407

A selection of bedroom and other furniture from G. Maddox's catalogue of 1882.

Top left: A kneehole dressing table, "in best deal and white china knobs, on castors".

Price Range: *£15 – £25 (in 1882 it was £2.15.0.)*

Top right: A 3ft. chest of drawers "in best deal with white china knobs".

Price Range: *£15 – £25 (in 1882 it was £2.16.0.)*

Centre left: A deal pedestal dressing table with nine drawers, again fitted with china knobs. This would now be sold as a partners or kneehole desk for a study, after the back rail to the top had been removed. *Original cost, £4. Nowadays the Price Range:* *£30 – £35*

Centre left: A deal chamber cupboard

Priceless. (50p.)

Centre right: A deal "tallboy" chest with china knobs.

Price Range: *£30 – £50*

Bottom left: A "best" deal towel horse, originally sold for six shillings. Unwanted in the main.

Available for shillings in junk shops.

Bottom right: A 3ft. 6ins. deal chest of plain desing, like the others.

Price Range: *£15 – £25*

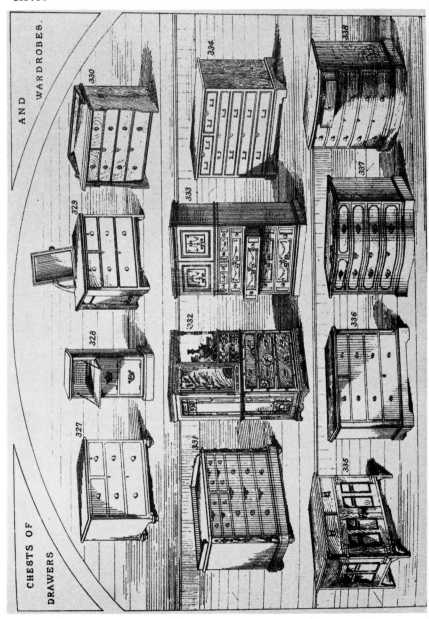

CHESTS OF DRAWERS AND WARDROBES.

CH408

A selection of typical chests of drawers (and wardrobes) from Shool-bred's Design book of 1876. Many represent types made from the 1860s on to the end of the century. Taking them from the top row, the following comments apply:-

Top row, left. A small chest similar to CH401. Made in mahogany, pine or oak.

Price Range: £15 – £25
Value Points: Few

Top row, left centre. A bedside cabinet/chest. Useful perhaps, but without merit aesthetically.

Price Range: £5 – £10

Top row, right centre. A dressing chest with mirror. The sides show a vague tendency to "joined" designs.

Price Range: £8 – £12

Top row, right. Another vaguely "joined" chest with a wooden gallery round the top.

Price Range: £10 – £15

Centre row, left. A higher quality chest with split balusters applied to the chamfered corners.

Price Range: £10 – £20

Centre row, centre. Two wardrobes, decorated with inlay or painted.

Price Range: £30 – £40

Centre row, right. A bracket-foot chest of mid-18th century design. Good proportion.

Price Range: £30 – £50

Bottom row, left. A panelled chest of vaguely pre-Art Nouveau design. Not popular at present.

Price Range: £10 – £20

Bottom row, left centre. Another rather 18th century design of good proportion.

Price Range: £20 – £30

Bottom row, right centre. A serpentine-front chest with inlaid banding. Nowadays, dealers might take off the solid apron around the bottom and "convert" the piece to an 18th century one.

Price Range: £60 – £90

Bottom row, right. Bow-fronted chest similar to CH400. A good piece.

Price Range: £25 – £40

No. 571. SOLID OAK CHEST OF DRAWERS 3 FT. WIDE.
JOINER-MADE, £8 15 0.

No. 522. SOLID OAK BACHELOR'S WARDROBE
3 FT. WIDE × 5 FT. 6 IN. HIGH.
JOINER-MADE, £12 15 0.

CH409

Back to William Morris's catalogue of the 1890s for a chest (left) in solid oak, proudly advertised as "joiner-made". The styling is simple but the top has the wooden gallery, with tapering sides, which seems to have been essential to Victorians, whether to retain their washing equipment or for other items, is not certain. On the right is a solid oak "bachelor's wardrobe" in which clothes could not possibly be hung, but which must have been useful for folded garments.

Price Range: *Chest (left)*   *£10 – £20*
             Wardrobe (right) £15 – £25

CH410

A late 19th century chest in the Hepplewhite style, i.e. with the splay
foot and bow-fronted. Usually of good quality, mahogany veneered in
plain or feathered woods, and made in large quantities. Many are still
available, but tend to be sold as 18th century pieces.

Price Range: *£40 – £80*

LIBRARY FURNITURE

The Victorians' love of literature and the heyday of the English written word gave rise to a reverence for the library or study in the house which has not been equalled since the first world war. Library furniture is now a remote speciality or a recent indulgence in campaign furniture; in the 19th century, library furniture was made in vast quantities, as a serious necessity for the responsible man. No new house design was complete without its library, study or "den" for the dominant paterfamilias. A man had to have a haven to which he could retire, remote and almost impregnable, in order to improve himself in study or to deal with the affairs of the day. To satisfy this enormous requirement, furniture manufacturers poured out huge numbers of tables, desks, chairs, bookshelves, bureaux and other pieces connected with books, papers and journals which no flickering screen has ever engendered. The section which follows deals all too briefly with this wonderful aspect of Victorian life and its furniture. The Englishman of the 1970s spends the lowest amount per head of any Western nation on books; it was not so in the 19th century, when both fiction and factual literature enjoyed a grip on the mind of the nation which was reflected in the abundance of the furniture designed to complement it.

L420

A mahogany desk of c.1840 with a full front above three long drawers.
Note that the wooden knob is well established. The turned decorative
pillars on either side are rather over-embellished and the ogee curve of
the top drawer front is unnecessary, but the matching of the figured
veneers is extremely professional. Inside the fall front the space is
divided between pigeon-holes and small drawers.

Price Range: *£125 – £160*
Value Points: *Exotic woods and veneers +++*

L421

A cylinder front mahogany bureau of c.1840, with a brass gallery around the top. The doors below the writing section are veneered in fine quality figured mahogany and conceal more drawers. The photograph showing the cylinder front raised reveals the drawers and pigeon-holes inside, where a slide may be drawn forward for writing purposes. This slide contains a leather-set section which may be inclined as shown. The front of the piece, beside the doors, is fluted and the feet are reeded. A fine quality piece of furniture.

Price Range: *£450 – £500*
Value Points: *Fine quality woods +++*
      Satinwood ++++

L422

A mahogany secretaire bookcase of c.1840, veneered in highly figured wood on the drawer and cupboard doors. The drawer section is deep in order to contain inner drawers and pigeon-holes — shown in the photograph of the piece in the open position. The writing space is lined with baize but could equally well be inset with tooled leather. The top clearly shows the shelves and the ridged grooves for adjusting their spacing.

Price Range: *£120 – £160*
Value Points: *Walnut +++*
       Figured mahogany ++

L423

A mid-Victorian Carlton House writing table in satinwood. Since the production of the original Carlton House design – in Hepplewhite's second edition of 1796 – this piece of furniture, with variations, has been reproduced extensively and is still being reproduced now. The use of satinwood is reserved for the higher quality versions, but many are made in mahogany. The example above is painted with male and female portraits, musical portraits, swags of this and that, flowers, etc.

Price Range: *Satinwood, £700 – £900*
                            Mahogany, £600 – £750

L424

A mahogany bookcase of c.1845 with spiral-turned columns on either side of the cupboard doors. Above the cupboard doors, in the lower section, there is a drawer with a convex front.

The glazed doors in the top are decorated with a carved moulding over the glass and this top section would have been fitted with shelves.

Price Range: £70 – £90

L425
A mid-19th century writing cabinet in a clearly "Sheraton" style with oval panels to the doors, reminiscent of Adam pieces. The cylinder top is raised to reveal the interior, where a slide may be drawn forward to provide greater writing space.
Price Range: *£175 – £225*

L426

A break-front bookcase of c.1840 with Gothic arching in the glazed upper door mouldings. Note the flattened arch of the lower door panels, so typical of the 1840s. The piece is of high quality, with lively mahogany veneers.

Price Range: £250 – £350

L427

A mahogany bookcase of the 1840–50 period with the typical arched panelling of the period. There are two drawers above the lower doors.
Price Range: *£60 – £80*

L428

A mid-Victorian oak library bookcase with panelled cupboards, the doors of which are decorated with mouldings in the 17th century style. It is highly carved, showing caryatids and lion masks as well as leaf and scroll decoration. An example of the Victorians' desire for "mediaeval" furniture.

Price Range: *£150 – £200*

L429

A burr walnut pedestal desk of c.1840, with brass ring handles. Note the thumbnail moulding around the top and the plain pedestal around the top and the plain pedestal around the bottom. The top is inset with leather.

Price Range: £180 – £230
Value Points: *Burr walnut or decorative veneers +++*

L430

A simpler pedestal desk of the 1840s with a leather top. This example is mounted on castors, evidently to satisfy a particularly mobile owner. The top is detachable from the pedestals and the back is boarded, i.e. not finished so as to stand centrally in a room. A partner's desk was originally one so large that it could accommodate an occupant (or partner) on each side, and hence was finished with drawers or cupboards on both sides. More often such centrally placed pedestal pieces of furniture were intended as library tables.

Price Range: *Partner's type, £140 – £180*
                Other   *£90 – £110*
Value Points: *Antique leather top ++*
                Decorative woods: *Walnut +++*
                                    figured mahogany ++
                                    Rosewood ++
                Original lock and Key +

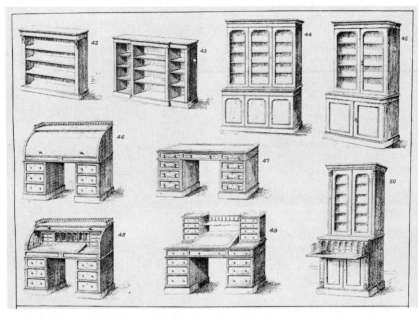

L431

A selection of library furniture from Shoolbred's design book of 1876, showing little progress in design from the 1840–50 period in the pieces displayed.

Price Range:

Top left.	*Bookcase*	*£15 – £25*
Top left centre.	*Bookcase (mahogany) (the break front adds to value)*	*£30 – £40*
Top right centre.	*Bookcase with glazed upper doors in mahogany*	*£80 – £100*
Top right.	*Bookcase with glazed upper doors in mahogany*	*£60 – £100*
Centre, left.	*Cylinder front pedestal desk*	*£100 – £150*
Centre, right.	*Oak pedestal desk*	*£70 – £85*
Bottom left.	*Cylinder front pedestal desk, shown open*	*£100 – £150*
Bottom centre.	*Pedestal desk with sloping writing surface, and drawers above*	*£70 – £90*
Bottom right.	*Secretaire bookcase in mahogany*	*£120 – £160*

L432
A mahogany bookcase of c.1845 flanked by columns which are carved with leaf decoration at the top. A well made and pleasantly proportioned piece.
Price Range: *£70 – £90*

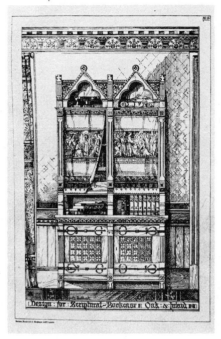

L433B

Two designs from Talbert's *Gothic Forms* of 1867, showing (left) a Scriptural bookcase in oak with inlays and (right) a cabinet. Observe the similarity of the bookcase to the photograph (opposite) of the bookcase by R. Norman Shaw exhibited in 1862 and now reposing in the Victoria and Albert Museum. All the pieces show a preoccupation with inlays, complicated locks and hinges, "joined" construction and enormous size. Visitors to the Hanley Read Collection Exhibition at the Royal Academy in 1872 will find similarity of form.

Such pieces appear on the market but rarely, and would tend to be the speciality of Sotheby's Belgravia auction rooms more than of a specialist dealer. Current taste for these items is not widespread.

One would hazard a suitable price range as being from £900 up to perhaps £1,000.

L434

A selection of "library" chairs from Wyman's Pattern Book of 1877. Note the frequent use of the Gothic motif – suitably serious and with the slightly religious overtones necessary for library atmosphere in the late 19th century. The seats must have been fitted with squab cushions unless the chairs were for ornamental purposes only. The wood used was normally oak or stained beech or birch.

Price Range:

Top row.		*£8 – £12 each*
Middle row.	*Single chairs,*	*£8 – £12*
	Armchair (centre),	*£15 – £20*
Bottom row.	*Ladder-chair, shown open (left)*	
	and closed (centre)	*£30 – £40*
	Single, hall-type chair	*£5 – £10*

L435

An octagonal table, probably intended for library use, on four fluted legs and a crossed base on castors. The top has an ebonised band around it; the rest of the table appears to be in walnut. Put at a date c.1870 but also similar in form to tables of the mid 1880s as shown in L436 overleaf.

Price Range: *£150 – £200*
Value Points: *Walnut +++*

No. 9 No. 11

L436

A selection of library furniture from Heal's catalogue of 1884, showing tables similar in form to L435 overleaf. Individual details as follows:-

Top left.   *A pedestal writing table with a shelf on top, made in mahogany, walnut or oak. The open gallery type of top detracts from price at present.*
             Price Range: £60 – £80

Top right.   *A more traditional pedestal writing table or desk with small drawers and gallery on top. Also made in mahogany, walnut or oak.*
             Price Range: £70 – £90

Bottom left. *A library table, with drawers in the frame. Many of these tables have been "converted" to 18th century library or "rent" tables by replacing the under structure with a centre pedestal base of 18th century type.*
             Price Range: £90 – £110

Bottom centre. *A cylinder fall writing table or desk with drawers and pigeon-holes inside.*
             Price Range: £100 – £150
             Value Points: Walnut +++

Bottom right. *Another library table, but without drawers. Otherwise similar to the example on the left.*
             Price Range: £70 – £90

Note!   *All the above pieces were made in walnut, mahogany or oak. The walnut used, however, in the solid, was often an American walnut of little figure and plain brown appearance.*

L437

A late 19th century pedestal writing table or desk with drawers on top
and a brass gallery. The piece is made in mahogany with a decorative
crossbanding of slightly "Sheraton" inspiration.
Price Range: *£120 – £150*

L438
A late 19th century writing table on square tapering legs with drawers
and a brass gallery on top. Again of "Sheraton" inspiration but with
considerable elegance and reserve in execution. The wood is mahogany
with a double stringing line inlaid in boxwood.
Price Range: *£150 – £250*

L439

A late 19th century bureau bookcase in mahogany, with satinwood crossbanding and an inlaid marquetry design in the fall. Note the quarter-round "shell" inlays in the corners of the drawers. The whole piece owes its design to the late 18th century and shows how the late Victorian taste had come full circle.

Price Range:　　*£250 – £350*
Value Points:　　*Small size +++*
　　　　　　　　(less than 3 ft. wide)

L440

A late 19th century mahogany kneehole desk, with a brushing slide under the top. The piece is virtually a straight reproduction of an 18th century Sheraton desk or dressing table, with satinwood quarter "shell" inlays in the corners of every drawer. The shaped apron in the kneehole space is, in fact, another shallow drawer. The piece is on bracket feet but was subsequently raised on castors to cater for that mobility of furniture considered so essential in the period.

Price Range: £280 – £350

L441

Library furniture from a William Morris catalogue of c.1900. The top two pieces are reproductions of late 18th or early 19th century book-cases, that on the right being fitted with a secretaire drawer, like L422. Many of these late 19th century pieces are now sold as earlier furniture or the tops are used for "marrying" with a mahogany fall-front bureau to produce an 18th century bureau bookcase for the export trade.

The two lower pieces are a mahogany dwarf bookcase (left) and a dwarf chest (right) both made in an 18th century style.

Price Range:

Top left,	*Bookcase/cabinet*	*£80 – £100*
Top right,	*Secretaire/cabinet*	*£120 – £140*
Bottom left,	*Dwarf bookcase*	*£12 – £18*
Bottom right,	*Dwarf chest*	*£15 – £25*

The Library

No. 247.—CHIPPENDALE MAHOGANY BOOKCASE, 8 ft. wide, fitted with cupboards, drawers, adjustable shelves and lattice work doors, and with an elegantly moulded cornice.
Price £29 18s. 6d.

No. 248.—SOLID WALNUT BOOKCASE, with enclosed secretaire, 4 ft. wide; also made in Fumed Oak or Mahogany. Price £11 11s. The same design with cupboards instead of secretaire below, price £7 18s. 6d.

No. 249.—MAHOGANY DWARF BOOKCASE, with adjustable shelves, made in any size. Price, from £6 15s. A less expensive quality, price, from £5 15s.

No. 25 .—BOOKCASE, in Mahogany, Walnut, or Fumed Oak, with shelves, cupboard, and drawer. Price £5 6 .

No. 251.—BOOKCASE, in Fumed Oak, Walnut, or Mahogany, with cupboards and drawer. Price £12 12s.

43

L442

Five bookcases from Norman & Stacey's catalogue of 1900–1910.

Top, left,   A straight forward reproduction of a Chippendale mahogany breakfront bookcase, with a broken pediment above. Known in the trade nowadays as "half-age" to denote old reproductions very near to the real thing in appearance.

Price Range: £100 – £150

Top, right,   The Edwardian version of a secretaire bookcase, with typical Edwardian cornice of semi-broken pediment type. The carved doors are typical of work in American walnut although the piece was also made in mahogany and fumed oak.

Price Range: £80 – £120

Bottom row,   Left. A mahogany dwarf bookcase with blind fretted decoration, square tapering feet.

Price Range: £10 – £20

Bottom row,   Centre. A fussy Edwardian design bookcase with a cupboard, drawer, turned gallery, and brackets under the top, which is wider than the main shelves.

Price Range: £10 – £20

Bottom row,   Right. Art Nouveau bookcase with a cupboard and drawer, a curtained alcove, upper shelves and cupboard with flat wooden gallery across the top. Note the flat Perpendicular arching and the long mediaeval hinges to the cupboard.

Price Range: £15 – £20

L444

A piece made by Gillow's in the 1870–90 period, showing the Japanese style which was popular then. The working of the pierced hinge and metal back plates on the handles, quite apart from the clearly Japanese decoration in the centre panels, and the square corner brackets, makes this a very classic example of the Japanese taste.

Price Range: *This piece, actually signed and numbered 1668 by Gillow's, was sold at Sotheby's Belgravia for £250 in October 1971.*

L445

A late Victorian or early Edwardian cylinder-front bureau in the style known as "Edwardian Sheraton". Apart from the Gothic arching of the gallery around the top, the ivory and boxwood inlaid decoration uses classical motifs in the Adam tradition. Note, however, the turned finials which are used to terminate the centre frame verticals and which are also used on the top corners of the gallery. These finials – see the whatnot section – appear to have been irresistible to Victorian manufacturers. The slide, on which the baize inner writing surface is to be found, pulls out to provide more writing space.

Price Range: *£80 – £120*

No. 264.　　　No. 265.

No. 263.—BOOKCASE BUREAU in Fumed Oak, with metal mounts, cupboards, drawers, and shelves at each end. Price £19 19s.

No. 264.—FUMED OAK WRITING TABLE, with leather top. Price £3 17s. 6d.

No. 265.—ARMCHAIR in Fumed Oak, in any shade of leather. Price £3 5s.

No. 266.—BOOKCASE in Fumed Oak, with cupboards, shelves and drawers. A unique design. Price £12 12s.

No. 266.

No. 267.—MAHOGANY TEA TABLE, with coloured tile top. Price from £3 12s. 6d.

No. 268.—HALF PEDESTAL WRITING TABLE, 4 ft. wide, in Walnut, Fumed Oak, or Mahogany. Leather top in any shade. Price £6 15s. 6d.

No. 269.—INLAID FUMED OAK BOOKCASE, with adjustable shelves, glass doors and metal mounts. Price £12 18s. 6d.

No. 270.—WRITING BUREAU in Inlaid Fumed Oak. Price £8 17s.

No. 271.—LIBRARY CHAIR, in Fumed Oak, Walnut, or Mahogany, and covered in morocco in any shade. Price £5 18s. 6d.

No. 272.—WRITING BUREAU in Fumed Oak, with cupboards, shelves, and drawers. Price £8 8s.

45

L446

Some library furniture from Norman & Stacey's catalogue of the 1900–1910 period, showing how the Art Nouveau influence had established itself.

Top row,	Left. A bureau bookcase, in fumed oak, of Art Nouveau inspiration, with metal mounts and shelves set into each end. *Price Range: £30 – £45*
Top row,	Left centre. A fumed oak writing table with a leather top. *Price Range: £15 – £20*
Top row,	Right centre. A fumed oak armchair. *Price Range: £5 – £10*
Top row,	Right. A fumed oak bookcase of "unique" design in the Art Nouveau manner. *Price Range: those that have survived would cost £10–£15*
Centre,	Left. A mahogany tea table with a coloured tile top and spindly legs of quaint arrangement. *Price Range: £5 – £10*
Centre,	Right. A half pedestal writing table made in walnut, fumed oak or mahogany, with a leather top. *Price Range: £10 – £20*
Bottom row,	Left. An inlaid fumed oak bookcase with metal mounts. *Price Range: £20 – £30*
Bottom row,	Left centre. A fumed oak writing bureau, on spindly cabriole legs, of Queen Anne inspiration. *Price Range: £20 – £30*
Bottom row,	Right centre. A library chair, covered in leather. *Price Range: £25 – £30*
Bottom row,	Right. A bureau in fumed oak, with a cupboard and shelves above. *Price Range: £15 – £20*

L447

A writing desk in American walnut with carved cupboard doors below, shown both open and closed. The handles are original, but the leather writing surface appears to have been renewed. Despite its piano-like appearance when closed it is a highly functional piece of furniture and is extremely well made. 1890–1900.

Price Range: £70 – £90

L448

Two writing tables from the same William Morris catalogue, illustrating vividly the contrast to be found in the 1890s. The top example is a design by W.A.S. Benson, made in fumed oak or green-stained ash according to the buyer's taste. It has many of the features to be found in contemporary design, particularly the shaping of the aprons and the mixture of panelled and turned column support to the writing surface. It is a design which aims at simplicity and yet in use will look a mess.

The lower example is a sophisticated 18th century reproduction, veneered in mahogany and with concave surfaces to the cupboards and drawers. These cupboards and drawers are included back and front i.e. it is a "partner's" desk or library table designed to stand centrally.

Price Range: *It is interesting to contrast the original prices (£9.15.0. for the top and £58 for the bottom) with those to-day:-*
Upper writing table, £30 − £40
Lower pedestal or partner's desk, £250 − £350.

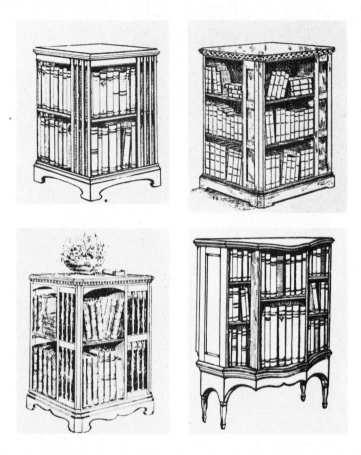

L449

Three revolving bookcases and a dwarf bookcase with a shaped front (bottom right) from a William Morris catalogue of c.1900. There are designs and pieces which have been reproduced up to the present day.

Price Range: *Revolving bookcases,*   *£20 – £30*
          Dwarf bookcase,   *£15 – £20*

DAVENPORTS

The name of the Davenport is assumed to have arisen from Gillow's Cost Books in the late 18th century, when the entry "Captain Davenport, a desk" occurs alongside a piece of furniture of this design. The sloping lid and gallery − brass or wood − around the top are characteristic, as are the real drawers on one side and the false on the other.

Ten years ago £20 would have bought the finest quality Davenport the market could offer. Now sums of over £300 are paid for Regency examples, and the Davenport, like the Canterbury, is in danger of becoming an over-priced piece of furniture. The examples which follow may all be assumed to have the following value points:-

Exotic Woods: *Satinwood ++++*
                    Burr walnut +++
                    Amboyna ++

Brass gallery ++
Secret drawers and complicated pigeon-holes or interior fittings ++

D460

A mahogany Davenport of 1830–40 period with turned column supports. The lid is inset with tooled leather and there is a rather interesting curved-section solid wooden gallery around the top. On this example the drawers are on the left; the false fronts are out of sight on the right hand side.

Price Range: *£140 – £180*

D461

A rosewood Davenport similar to the previous example but with carved leaf decoration at the top of the columns. On this example the drawers down the right hand side are enclosed by a door, this enabling all four of them to be locked up "at a stroke". Note the little ink-pot drawer let in to the right hand side of the top.

Price Range: £120 – £160

D462

A mahogany Davenport showing the hinged "inkpot" drawer at the side
in the open position. The slide beneath it is also shown open. The
squared restraint of the design would lead to a Regency description but
the flat bun feet indicate a date of c.1840.

Price Range: £250 – £300

D463
A Victorian walnut Davenport with a brass gallery on the top, folding writing surface and four rather well-graduated drawers below. Almost Georgian in its severity and for that reason considered more desirable — and hence expensive. Would probably be sold as "Regency".
Price Range: *£300 – £350*

D464

A burr walnut Davenport of the 1850–60 period on which the scrolled and carved front supports follow the curvilinear design of other furniture of the period. There is a brass gallery around the top and the inlaid stringing lines are developed into floral decoration at the corners.

Price Range: *£200 – £250*

D465

Another walnut Davenport, similar to the previous example but with a serpentine front edge to the top and without stringing or other inlays. The walnut veneer is lightly figured, verging on the burr variety, and there is no brass gallery.

Price Range: £150 – £200

D466

A Davenport in the manner of the Great Exhibition pieces of the 1850s and 1860s. It is in amboyna wood with ebonised banding and inlaid with plaques of Wedgwood or other manufacture in blue and white relief. The fluted columns are topped with metal mounts in ormolu. The sloping lid is inset with tooled leather and there is a brass gallery around the top. An unusual example, involving fine craftsmanship.

Price Range: *£275 – £350*

D467

A walnut Davenport of c.1860 with a fretted gallery around the top. Note that the ink-pot drainer has been opened and pivots on a hinge for use when writing. Again the drawers down the right hand edge of the piece are enclosed by a door. The columns are fluted to half-way down and then, after a bun, break out into spiral turning.

Price Range: *£150 – £200*

D468
A fine quality walnut Davenport, with a cylinder front (sometimes known as a "piano" top). There is a rising compartment, shown in the risen position here, at the top, containing three small drawers and four pigeon holes. This whole section can be pushed down and retained by a spring-loaded catch. The open lid reveals a sloping writing surface of adjustable type, covered in leather, which folds flat to enable the writing surface to be closed and pushed inwards on its slides before the cylinder lid is closed. The "cabriole" type columns at the front are carved with leaf and scroll decoration.
Price Range: £320 – £360

D469

A late Victorian mahogany Davenport, c.1890, with a pierced wooden gallery. The handles on the drawers may be a replacement; certainly they show the influence of the Art Movement. The turning of the columns is simple and perhaps too reminiscent of cheap mass-production work.

Price Range: *£80 – £100*

D470

An unusual mid-Victorian Davenport desk on a turned stand with scroll feet. The absence of the normal body of the desk with its drawers makes this less desirable functionally.

Price Range: £75 – £100

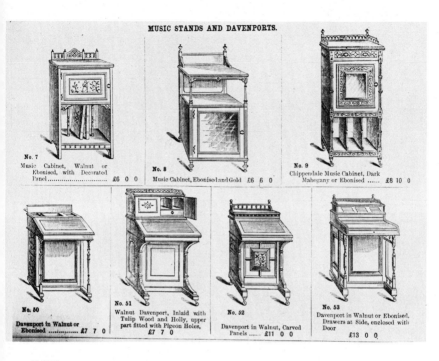

MUSIC STANDS AND DAVENPORTS.

No. 7
Music Cabinet, Walnut or Ebonised, with Decorated Panel.................................. £6 0 0

No. 8
Music Cabinet, Ebonised and Gold £6 6 0

No. 9
Chippendale Music Cabinet, Dark Mahogany or Ebonised £8 10 0

No. 50
Davenport in Walnut or Ebonised £7 7 0

No. 51
Walnut Davenport, Inlaid with Tulip Wood and Holly, upper part fitted with Pigeon Holes, £7 7 0

No. 52
Davenport in Walnut, Carved Panels £11 0 0

No. 53
Davenport in Walnut or Ebonised. Drawers at Side, enclosed with Door £13 0 0

D471

A page from Heal's catalogue of 1884 illustrating Davenports and music stands. The four Davenports shown, on the bottom row, exhibit the characteristics of the later, mass-produced items particularly in the use of machine-turned columns. All the examples shown were available in walnut, but three were also available in ebonised finish as an alternative. That on the right has a "piano" top.

Price Range: *Walnut,*   *£90 – £120*
                 Ebonised,   *£70 – £100*
The music stands' price would be £20 – £30

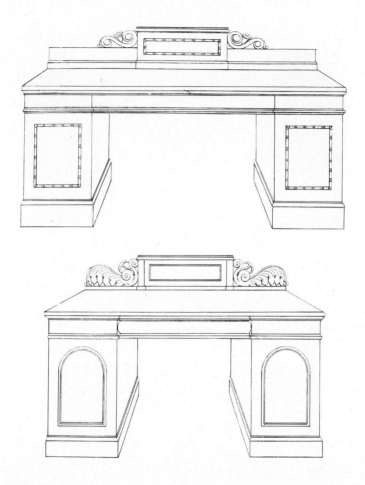

S480

Two sideboards from T. King's *Modern Style of Cabinet Work* of 1829, which show forms used into the beginning of the Victorian era. Both would have been made in mahogany. They have the merit of relative simplicity compared with the over-exuberance of the 1845–55 period, and the smaller versions are recovering popularity after a considerable period of lack of interest by collectors.

Price Range: *£110 – £150*
Value Points: *Small size (4ft. long or under) +++*

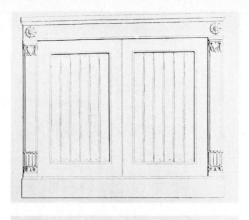

S481

Another two designs from the *Modern Style of Cabinet Work* of 1829, which show forms which remained popular up to the 1840s. The upper, and simpler, example owes much more to what is considered to be the Regency in style whereas the lower would be classified as virtually Victorian by many dealers. So much so, in fact, that the arching of the panelled doors would be "straightened" by a restorer, i.e. cut square like those in the upper version in order to be sure of selling the piece as a Regency example.

A favourite modification, in addition to the cutting of the arches, is to fit a brass lattice in front of the material in the door panels, thus catering completely for the satisfaction of modern taste in what is accepted as "Regency" design.

Price Range: £110 – £160

S482

A mahogany sideboard or chiffonier of c.1840, with figured veneers in the door panels and mounted on reeded bun feet. The heavily machine-carved top rail with its scrolling would almost certainly be removed by many dealers, who would not find it difficult to sell the piece as late Regency from the top shelf downwards. The piece might even be lightened by removing the veneered door panels and replacing them with the regulation brass lattice and silk material of earlier pieces.

Price Range: £60 – £80

S483
A simpler mahogany sideboard of the early Victorian period, 1840–45.
The construction is of fairly cheap pine or deal veneered with decoratively figured mahogany. The convex front to the drawers seems to have been very popular at the time.
Price Range: £80 – £120

S484

A more sophisticated early Victorian sideboard with columns decorating the front and the machine-carved top rail and brackets resembling those of S482. Again the door panels are decorated with figured mahogany veneers, and the fact that these panels are square would lend to easier "conversion" to more popular forms of modern "Regency".

Price Range: *£80 – £120*

S485

Two designs from Henry Wittaker's *Cabinet Maker's and Upholsterer's Treasury of Designs* of 1847, showing how the earlier simplicity was disappearing into extraordinarily elaborate forms. These pieces were designed to be about seven feet long and must have been extremely expensive, if they were practically executed. Despite the felicity of both mirror frames, modern dealing practice would probably be to remove the mirrors and frames and to sell the lower half as a sideboard or chiffonier while using the mirror frame as a highly decorative surround for a padded bed-head.

Price Range: £80 – £120

S486

The bottom half of a piece of furniture which is a cross between a side-board and a whatnot. The example in the photograph is missing its upper shelves, supported on turned columns similar to those in the lower portion. The piece is light and cheerful; even though it is cheaply made, the thin burr walnut veneers and the mirror inset in the door give it a pleasant elegance.

Price Range: £25 – £35

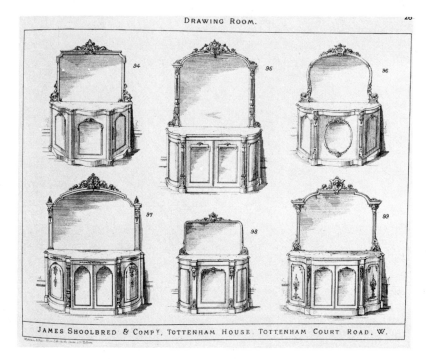

JAMES SHOOLBRED & COMPY, TOTTENHAM HOUSE, TOTTENHAM COURT ROAD, W.

S487

A page from Shoolbred's catalogue of 1876 showing a variety of chiffoniers intended for drawing room — not dining room — use. The comparison with S488 overleaf, showing dining room pieces, is interesting. The pieces illustrated above are lighter, have greater areas of mirror, and the corners are all carved as serpentine in shape. If one looks at these and then the examples in S488 et seq., the question "What has happened to the upper mirrors?" springs to the lips. Several of these types would have had white marble tops.

Price Range: *£80 – £120, but see S489 et seq.*

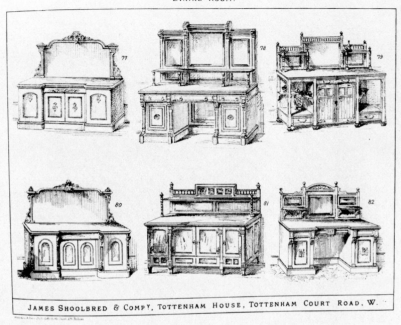

JAMES SHOOLBRED & COMPY, TOTTENHAM HOUSE, TOTTENHAM COURT ROAD, W.

S488

Dining room pieces from Shoolbred's catalogue of 1876. Conspicuously less elegant and desirable than the drawing room furniture in S487. Indeed these sideboards are quite ponderous and, in several cases, fussy without achieving lightness of form. Whether the rectangularity and heavier nature of this furniture was intended to convey a more solemn atmosphere to the serious business of eating is hard to say, but the overall impression is depressing.

Price Range: £50 – £120

S489
A side cabinet or chiffonier of 1860—70 date in walnut with amboyna banding and marquetry inlaid. The mounts on the two front columns are of brass. The stringing lines and the marquetry are in ivory. The top is ebonised.
Price Range: *£200 — £250*

S490

A walnut and marquetry side cabinet or chiffonier of c.1860. This piece is of clearly much higher quality than S489, although similar in basic design. The ormolu mounts are more detailed and the marquetry, instead of a development of stringing lines into a design, is conceived as a floral decoration involving different woods to achieve an intricate and varied effect which adds considerably to the value.

Price Range: *£500 – £600*

S491

Another side cabinet, c.1860, in which the marquetry is again more developed than that of S489 and S490. The basic background veneer is again walnut but the centre doors are ebonised and the floral marquetry is even more detailed. Beneath the marquetry urns the scrolled decoration is inlaid in ivory. The metal mounts are again very detailed, apart from being more numerous, and the gadrooning around the top and base edges is of metal stamping.

Price Range: *£1200 – £1500*

JAMES SHOOLBRED & COMPY, TOTTENHAM HOUSE, TOTTENHAM COURT ROAD, W.

S492
Another page of drawing room furniture from Shoolbred's 1876 catalogue. Note the similarity of the top left hand example to S489 and S490. These pieces were clearly costly and involved considerable craftsmanship with detailed inlaying.

The lower row shows simpler pier cabinets with metal or carved mounts.

Price Range: *Top row. Credenzas, £200 – £600. See S489 & 490. Bottom row. Pier cabinets, £100 – £175. See S493 and 494.*

S493

A walnut double-door display cabinet with fluted columns decorating the corners. The mounts at the top of the columns are ormolu and there is an ormolu metal strip down the front door edge. The veneered surfaces are edged with stringing lines in boxwood and ebony.

Price Range: *£180 – £250*

S494

A typical mid-Victorian display cabinet in walnut with metal mounts and boxwood inlays. The moulding around the top has been ebonised. These pieces were made in considerable quantities and it is only recently that their decorative value has become widely appreciated. In later years they were produced in totally ebonised form.

Price Range: *£90 – £110. (Walnut).*

N.B. The ebonised versions are much less popular and would be in the £40 – £60. range.

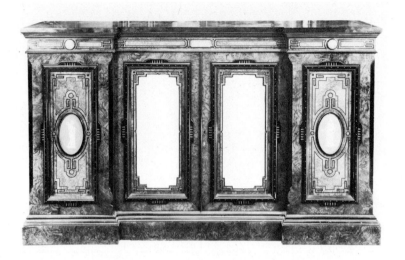

S495
A side cabinet in walnut and amboyna with ebony stringing and inlaid "Wedgwood" plaques as well as mirrored centre doors. Victorian cabinet makers lavished much fine workmanship on such pieces, but the main demand for them appears to be in the export trade.
Price Range: £150 – £200

S496

A burr walnut sideboard with ivory and boxwood inlays and a white marble top. The turned baluster gallery around the top is perhaps a bit weak from a design point of view, and the different shapes of the mirrors in the top compared to those below makes for a lack of coherence which would tempt one to remove the top entirely.

Price Range: *£100 – £150.*

S497

A satinwood sideboard of late 19th century date, possibly 1870–90. showing a return to classical 18th century influences in design. The bow centre doors with oval panels and the square tapering feet are reminiscent of Adam and Sheraton designs. Again the degree of workmanship is very fine and the choice of satinwood veneers in impeccable.

Price Range: £350 – £400

Value points: *This is a satinwood piece and hence well above the price range for other woods.*

S498
Two sideboards from a William Morris catalogue of c.1900 which go to
show that high quality reproductions of 18th century sideboards have
been with us for a long time. The upper example was sold as an
"Hepplewhite" version whereas that below was described as "Sheraton".
These "half-age" pieces are now in considerable demand for export
dealers.
Price Range: £100 – £150

S499

Two oak "sideboards" from the same William Morris catalogues. These
dressers represent the desire to return to earlier and simpler forms of
Tudor and other inspiration. The wood was left unstained and in its
natural state, which is extremely dull.

The upper example is an adaption in design from original 17th century
dressers. Features which include the scalloped central arch in the top
and the leaded glass doors are 19th century additions to the original
concept.

The lower example is possibly closer to the original 17th and early
18th century dressers it emulates, but the Art Nouveau influence has
provided the shaping of the back uprights and the sharp squareness of
the overall outline.

Price Range:	*Upper,*	*£40 – £60*
	Lower,	*£50 – £70*

S500
A late 19th century or even Edwardian rosewood sideboard, heavily inlaid with ivory marquetry and incorporating a wealth of shelves, turned columns and mirrors, all topped by a broken pediment.
Price Range: *£60 – £80*

S501

A sideboard of c.1900 made in American walnut and exhibiting much machine carving in bas-relief. There is really very little one can say to describe this piece; the two bulging drawers appear to have been inspired by the side-turret design of contemporary warships. Ghastly.

Price Range: *£10 – £25*

No. 224—INLAID MAHOGANY CHINA CABINET Price £14 18s. 6d.

No. 225—INLAID MAHOGANY CHINA CABINET Price £11 11s.

No. 226—INLAID MAHOGANY CURIO CASE. Price £7 18s. 6d.

No. 222—INLAID MAHOGANY SHERATON CHINA CABINET Price £9 9s.

No. 228.—MAHOGANY CABINET Finely carved, 4 ft. wide. Price £14 15s.

No. 229—DARK MAHOGANY CABINET, Price £16 16s.

No. 23 DARK MAHOGANY CABINET, 4 ft. wide Price £5 18s. 6d.

40

S502

An almost nightmare page from Norman & Stacey's catalogue of Edwardian period. The upper row of china and curio cabinets are at least based on late 18th century design, but the lower row advances upon one like creatures from a Hammer Films' production. Who was responsible for this outbreak, or where it originated, is impossible to find out; Norman & Stacey cannot be blamed entirely, for many other manufacturers turned out these flimsily made horrors.

It is beyond the author's imagination to price them.

S503
Another incredible piece from the 1900-1910 decade — this time a corner display cabinet — which shows all the characteristics of furniture from a house of ill-frame ebonised for respectable parlour use.
Price Range: *This one was £30; suit yourself.*

S504

A display cabinet of c.1890 in mahogany with satinwood inlaid banding.
It is considerably restrained and has an affinity with 18th century
design, particularly in the astragal moulding decorating the glass door.
Price Range: *£35 – £50*

S505

An ornate display cabinet of c.1900, showing many Art Nouveau motifs,
such as the heart shaped fretting of the top gallery. The metalwork
appears to have been specially made, in particular the hinges, and the
inlaying is of a particularly high quality. Clearly this is very much a
craftsman piece of individual design quite distinct from the mass production of, say, Norman and Stacey, whose furniture, nevertheless,
follows similar outlines in many cases.

Price Range: *Individual pieces such as this, in which Sotheby's Belgravia have specialised, are difficult to price. It is unlikely
that such pieces could be obtained for less than £400
nowadays.*

S506

A Buhl or Boulle side cabinet with metal mounts. André Charles Boulle was a French artist of the Louis XIV period and originated this form of marquetry made from shell and metal. It was very popular in the Regency period in England and was reproduced in various items of furniture in the 19th century, with side cabinets and tables particularly prominent. The example above shows similarity with the designs of other side cabinets illustrated in photographs and design books. Much sought after by the Italian export trade.

Price Range: £450 – £600

S507
A Victorian reproduction oak dresser of traditional design. Due to the
high price of genuine early dressers there is now a considerable demand
for these pieces which have a certain mellowness of age in them.
Price Range: *£120 – £180*

S508

A splendid example of an oak Art Nouveau sideboard, perhaps crude by artist-craftsman standards, but nevertheless very genuine and very typical.

Price Range: *This piece was sold at Sotheby's Belgravia in June 1972 for £14. It was a snip. At that price, buy as many as you can and store them.*

W511

A rosewood whatnot of c. 1840 with simple shelving and a drawer under
the bottom shelf. The turned columns still show restraint in their sym-
metrical design and the piece owes its simplicity to Georgian influences.
Price Range: *£80 – £100*

W512

A mahogany whatnot of c. 1850. The shelves are still simple but the turning of the columns has become slightly more bulbous than that of W511 and the pointed turned finials on the top shelf, above the columns, are purely decorative. The fretwork on each side of the top shelf seems to have become more popular in the Victorian period, as the examples which follow show.

Price Range: £60 – £80

W513

A walnut corner whatnot with fretted decoration which has again suffered some damage. The turned column supports are stepped back at the front of the shelves for support, but the turned finials on the shelves above each front column are decorative only and are not part of the construction.

Price Range: *£60 – £80*

W514

A walnut whatnot supported by double turned columns and decorated with fretwork under the two middle shelves as well as the top. A foot is missing from the left hand of the lowest shelf, at the front.

Price Range: £50 – £70

W515

An unusual whatnot with very open spiral turned columns and marquetry inlaid shelves. The effect of fragile elegance achieved by the open spirals may be contrasted with the rather bulbous stolidity of some of the other examples.

Price Range: *£60 – £80*

W516
Another rosewood whatnot with spirally turned columns and a (broken again) fretted gallery around the top. The addition of a drawer adds to the desirability of the piece.
Price Range: £80 – £100

W517
A rosewood whatnot with a (broken) fretted gallery around the top, on turned columns. The three shelves are, in fact, veneered in rosewood and the turned columns are made in birch, or some other hardwood, which has been subsequently stained.
Price Range: *£50 – £70*

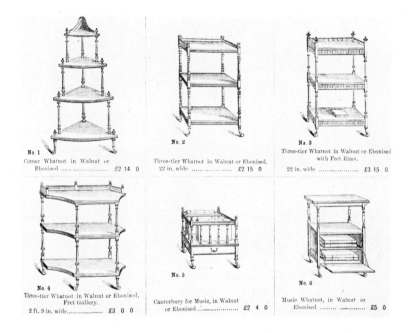

No. 1
Corner Whatnot in Walnut or Ebonised £2 14 0

No. 2
Three-tier Whatnot in Walnut or Ebonised. 22 in. wide £2 15 0

No. 3
Three-tier Whatnot in Walnut or Ebonised with Fret Rims. 22 in. wide £3 15 0

No. 4
Three-tier Whatnot in Walnut or Ebonised, Fret Gallery. 2 ft. 9 in. wide.................. £3 0 0

No. 5
Canterbury for Music, in Walnut or Ebonised £2 4 0

No. 6
Music Whatnot, in Walnut or Ebonised £5 0

W518
A page of whatnots (and a music Canterbury) from Heal's catalogue of 1884. They are all described as being available in walnut or ebonised. Even the corner whatnot is on castors.

The prices then ranged from £2.14.0. to £5.0.0. As readers of the preceding pages will have noted, prices now are from £60 to £100.

W519
A hall-type mahogany whatnot with its own built-in mirrors, which detract somewhat from its spirally achieved elegance. Note again the decorative finials on each shelf except the bottom.
Price Range: £40 – £60

CA520

A walnut Canterbury with twist-turned uprights and a drawer beneath.
Note that the feet are also twist-turned and that there is a little floral
marquetry inlay on the flat surface of the top rail.

Price Range: *£60–£90*

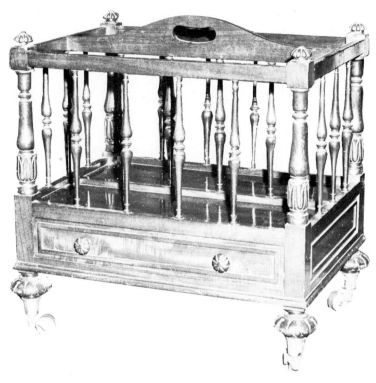

CA521

A mahogany Canterbury of 1840-50 with turned uprights and a fretted handle for carrying. The leaf carving and flat cheese-shaped buns above the castors are typical of the late Regency and early Victorian period.
Price Range: £70 – £90

CA522
A rosewood Canterbury of c. 1840 with fretted divisions and a drawer beneath. These Canterburies are more light-hearted and decorative than the turned upright divided type which follow the original 18th century layout.
Price Range: £80 – £100

CA523
A walnut Canterbury, similar in style to the previous example, but decorated with a painted scene depicting a bird and flowers.
Price Range: £80 − £100.

CA524

A papier-mâché music Canterbury of c.1860 decorated with mother of pearl and shell inlays. The pearl knobs on the convex-fronted drawer in the base may be seen in the floral inlay. A delightful piece of incidental furniture.

Price Range: *£150 – £200.*

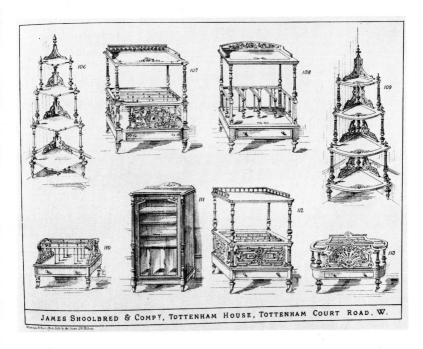

JAMES SHOOLBRED & COMP?, TOTTENHAM HOUSE, TOTTENHAM COURT ROAD, W.

CA525

A page of Canterburies (and two corner whatnots) from Shoolbred's catalogue of 1876. The form has developed an upper shelf in three cases and the use of fretwork has become universal.

Price Range: *Top row. Corner whatnots, see W513*
Top row. Canterburies, £60 – £95
Bottom row, left, £40 – £60
Bottom row, left centre, Music cabinet £40 – £70
Bottom row, right centre, £60 – £95
Bottom row, right, £40 – £60

CA526

A bamboo Canterbury of rather indeterminate date, probably pre-1914, but which could equally well have been made in the Colonies in the 1920s and 1930s. The handles on the drawer, if original, are an Art Nouveau design which was made in the 1880s and '90s. The painted decoration somehow does not match up to the space available for it; one finds it hard to believe that the parrot in the centre panel was intended to be partly decapitated by the edge of the panel.

Price Range: £20 – £40

CA527

A later Victorian ebonised Canterbury with an upholstered top. The balustraded gallery is typical of the 1880-1900 period (see the armchairs also) and the turning follows the later period in its decoration.

Price Range: £35 – £45

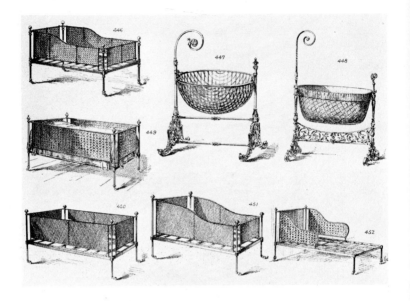

B540

A page from Children's swing cots and bedsteads from Shoolbred's catalogue of 1876. They are currently in vogue for use as jardiniéres, but clearly are highly decorative when made in brass. The swing cot bases would, however, be more likely to be in cast iron for stability, and hence painted.

Price Range: Bedsteads (Brass) £30 – £50
                 Swing Cots, £40 – £60

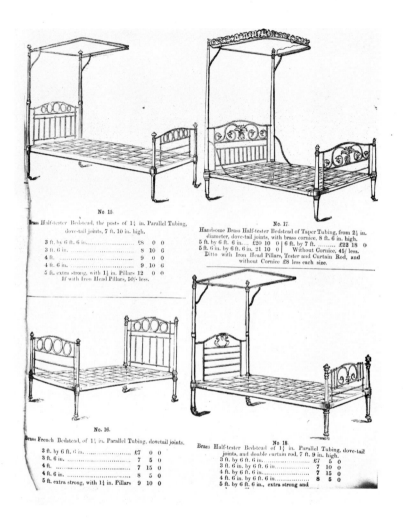

No. 15.

Brass Half-tester Bedstead, the posts of 1¼ in. Parallel Tubing, dove-tail joints, 7 ft. 10 in. high.

3 ft. by 6 ft. 6 in	...	£8	0	0
3 ft. 6 in.	...	8	10	6
4 ft.	...	9	0	0
4 ft. 6 in.	...	9	10	6
5 ft. extra strong, with 1¼ in. Pillars	12	0	0

If with Iron Head Pillars, 50/- less.

No. 17.

Handsome Brass Half-tester Bedstead of Taper Tubing, from 2¼ in. diameter, dove-tail joints, with brass cornice, 8 ft. 6 in. high.

5 ft. by 6 ft. 6 in.... £20 10 0 | 6 ft. by 7 ft. £22 18 0
5 ft. 6 in. by 6 ft. 6 in. 21 10 0 | Without Cornice, 45/ less.
Ditto with Iron Head Pillars, Tester and Curtain Rod, and without Cornice £8 less each size.

No. 16.

Brass French Bedstead, of 1¼ in. Parallel Tubing, dovetail joints.

3 ft. by 6 ft. 6 in.,	...	£7	0	0
3 ft. 6 in.	...	7	5	0
4 ft.	...	7	15	0
4 ft. 6 in.	...	8	5	0
5 ft. extra strong, with 1¼ in. Pillars	9	10	0

No. 18.

Brass Half-tester Bedstead of 1¼ in. Parallel Tubing, dove-tail joints, and double curtain rod, 7 ft. 9 in. high.

3 ft. by 6 ft. 6 in	...	£7	5	0
3 ft. 6 in. by 6 ft. 6 in	...	7	10	0
4 ft. by 6 ft. 6 in	...	7	15	0
4 ft. 6 in. by 6 ft. 6 in	...	8	5	0
5 ft. by 6 ft. 6 in., extra strong and			

B541

Brass half-tester bedsteads from George Maddox's catalogue of 1882, together with one standard bedstead (bottom, left). Very decorative and beloved of interior decorators.

Price Range: Brass half-testers   *Single, £40 – £60*
                                        double, £120 – £180
            Brass bedstead,   *Single, £20 – £40*
                                        double, £80 – £100

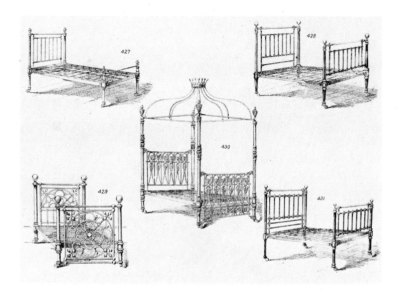

B542

A further page of beds from Shoolbred's catalogue of 1876 showing (centre) a highly decorative brass four-poster with surmounting canopy frame, finishing in a coronet.

Price Range: *£150 – £200*

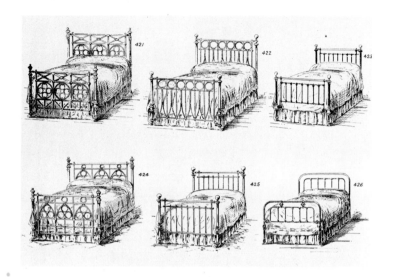

B543
Six varieties of double bedstead design, made either from brass or iron tubing. From Shoolbred's 1876 design book.
Price Range: Brass, £90 – £150
*   Iron, £20 – £40*

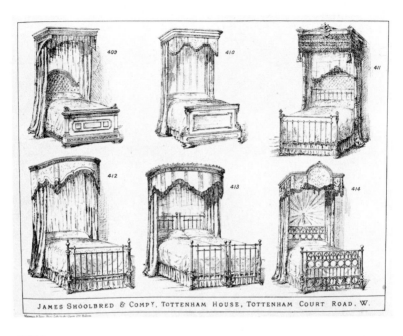

JAMES SHOOLBRED & COMPY, TOTTENHAM HOUSE, TOTTENHAM COURT ROAD, W.

B544

Six half-tester double bedsteads with drapes fitted. From Shoolbred's catalogue. The hangings are quite opulent and illustrate the way that the quite straightforward bed structure may be adorned.

Price Range: *Mahogany, £90 – £120*
                     Brass, £120 – £180

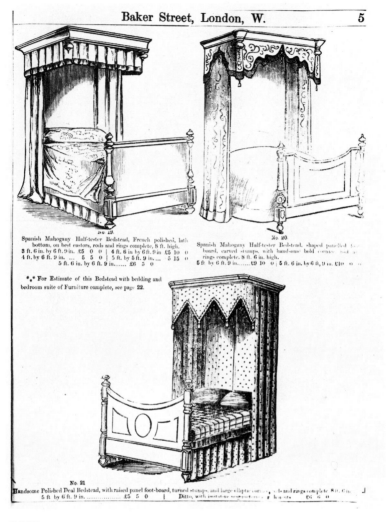

Spanish Mahogany Half-tester Bedstead, French polished, lath bottom, on best castors, rods and rings complete, 8 ft. high.
3 ft. 6 in. by 6 ft. 9 in. £5 0 0 | **4 ft. 6 in by 6 ft. 9 in.** £5 10 0
4 ft. by 6 ft. 9 in. ... 5 5 0 | **5 ft. by 5 ft. 9 in.** ... 5 15 0
5 ft. 6 in. by 6 ft. 9 in. £6 5 0

Spanish Mahogany Half-tester Bed-tead, shaped panelled foot board, carved stumps, with hand-ome bold corners, rod and rings complete, 8 ft. 6 in. high.
5 ft. by 6 ft. 9 in. ......£9 10 0 | **5 ft. 6 in. by 6 ft. 9 in.** £10 0 0

** For Estimate of this Bedstead with bedding and bedroom suite of Furniture complete, see page 22.

No. 21
Handsome Polished Deal Bedstead, with raised panel foot-board, turned stumps, and large elliptic corners, rods and rings complete 8 ft. 6 in.
5 ft. by 6 ft. 9 in. .... £5 5 0 | Ditto, with pantstors mountings... rods and rings £6 6 0

B545

Some simpler half-tester wooden bedsteads from Maddox's catalogue of 1882. These rely on typical turned uprights and simple panelling for decoration as far as the structure is concerned; the hangings do the rest.

Price Range: £90 – £120

B546

A page of bedroom furniture from Norman & Stacey's catalogue of the 1900–1910 period, showing four beds (bottom row) of which the two central examples are clearly Art Nouveau inspired. The fumed ash suite (top row) is also from the same stable, the tiles on the back of the washstand being particularly characteristic of the genre.

Price Range: *Washstands, £10 – £20*
Dressing chests, £15 – £25
Wardrobes, £10 -- £15
Beds, £8 – £15

B547
A clothes press of c.1840 in mahogany. The form is basically unaltered
from the late 18th century examples, consisting of a chest of drawers on
which a cupboard containing shelves has been mounted. The differences
are in the arched door panels, top moulding and the base plinth which
is used instead of bracket feet.
Price Range: *£30 – £40*

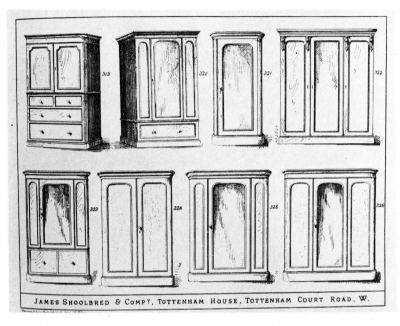

JAMES SHOOLBRED & COMPY, TOTTENHAM HOUSE, TOTTENHAM COURT ROAD, W.

B548

A clothes press and several wardrobes from Shoolbred's catalogue. The use of the shallow arched panel was evidently still popular after some 30 years.

Price Range:	*Clothes press, £30 − £40*
	Wardrobes, £10 − £50
Value Points:	*Decorative veneers ****
	Satinwood ****

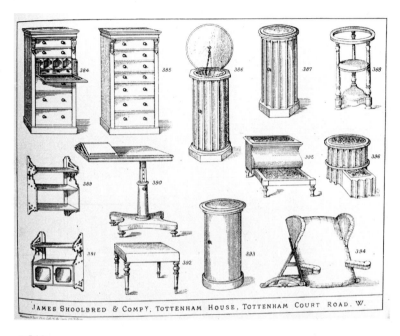

JAMES SHOOLBRED & COMPY, TOTTENHAM HOUSE, TOTTENHAM COURT ROAD. W.

B549
Essential items of bedroom furniture from Shoolbred's 1876 catalogue.
Top row, left. A Wellington chest, with secretaire drawers.
Price Range: £90 – £120
Wellington chest, without secretaire.
Price Range: £70 – £90
Other items. Commodes, pot holders, stool, bedside and reading table,
basin stand, shelves, backrest.
Price Range: From £5 – £40

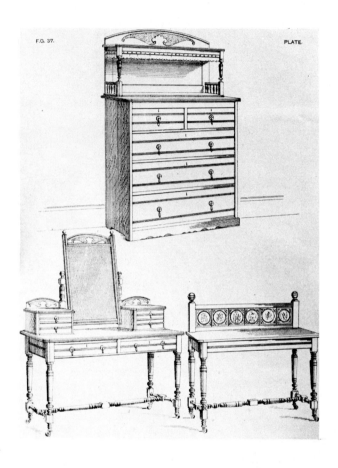

B550

A suite of bedroom furniture from the *Cabinet Makers' Pattern Book* of 1878, published by Wymans. The suite is described as being manufactured by Audas and Leggott of Hull. The use of the parallel grooving to lighten the drawer surfaces seems to have become common about 1865–1870.

Price Range: *Chest, £15 – £25*
          Dressing table, £15 – £25
          Washstand, £5 – £10

B551

An ugly dressing table of the 1870-80 period with an oval mirror and large reeded buns above fluted legs. The shaping and the flat platform base are difficult to understand. Shoolbred illustrated several in 1876, some with front legs of cabriole form. This piece is in mahogany.

Price Range: £10 – £20

B552

A dressing table designed by Owen Jones for Eynsham Hall, Oxon, in 1873. In fact Shoolbred's catalogue of 1876 shows examples very similar in design. This piece is in a pleasant, light wood and the stringing lines and neat black knobs contribute to an easy formality of design which is wholly missing from much furniture of the period. Unfortunately many dressing tables of this sort have had the top section removed to cater for the enormous trade in pedestal desks.

Price Range: £75 – £100

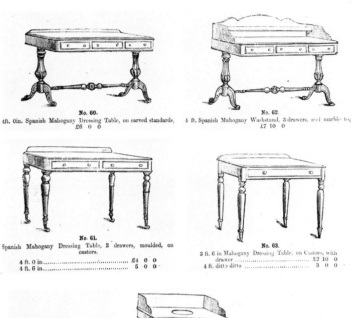

No. 60.
4ft. 0in. Spanish Mahogany Dressing Table, on carved standards,
£6 0 0

No. 62.
4 ft. Spanish Mahogany Washstand, 3 drawers, and marble top
£7 10 0

No. 61.
Spanish Mahogany Dressing Table, 2 drawers, moulded, on
castors.

4 ft. 0 in. £4 0 0
4 ft. 6 in. 5 0 0

No. 63.
3 ft. 6 in Mahogany Dressing Table, on Castors, with
drawer £2 10 0
4 ft. ditto ditto 3 0 0

No. 64.
Best Mahogany Washstand with Marble Top, on Castors.

3 ft. £2 15 0
3 ft. 6 in. 3 5 0
4 ft. 3 15 0

B553

Mahogany bedroom furniture from Maddox's catalogue of 1882. The top two pieces, a dressing table (left) and washstand (right) would now be considered suitable for conversion to writing table use. The other — turned leg — examples are less desirable, particularly that at the bottom with its marble top holed for basin location.

Price Range: Top row, £15 – £25
                 Middle row, £10 – £20
                 Bottom row, £5 – £10

B554
Two pot holders of differing design, the circular example being considered more desirable for conversion to a cheese box, record player
cabinet (45 r.p.m. records only), statue pedestal, bottle cache, or
whatever.
Price Range: *Square, £7 – £12*
                Round, £10 – £20

B555
Two bedside table-cum-commodes where again circularity attracts more than squareness.

Price Range: *Circular, £25 – £30*
                   Square, £5 – £15

B556
Wardrobes from William Morris & Co's catalogues of c.1900. Now considered almost totally undesirable except by immigrant furnishers.
Price Range: £5 – £10

B557
Two dressing tables in 18th century styles by William Morris & Co.,
c.1900. That on the right, a Sheraton style satinwood table with a
shield-shaped dressing glass on it (also in satinwood) is practically a
straight reproduction.

Price Range: Left (mahogany) £25 – £40
                   Right (satinwood) £40 – £60
                   "Shield" dressing glass in satinwood £20 – £30

B558
Two further bedside cabinets/pot holders, this time in satinwood, illustrating the late 18th century taste which the William Morris reproduction
furniture was catering for.
Price Range: £15 – £20

NO. 650. INLAID MAHOGANY WARDROBE. 6 FT. 9 IN. HIGH × 6 FT. WIDE.
£29 0 0.

No. 663. INLAID MAHOGANY "SHERATON" WARDROBE. 7 FT. HIGH.
£30 0 0.

B559
Two inlaid mahogany wardrobes from William Morris & Co.'s catalogue
of c. 1900. Both owe a great deal to 18th century design.
Price Range: £30 – £50

B560
An inlaid mahogany writing or dressing table of c. 1900. The design owes something to the Carlton House writing table and is quite elegant except for the oval mirror which provides too contrasting a shape.
Price Range: £80 – £120

B561
A dressing table straight out of Charles Addams, funereally ebonised.
Price Range: *£40 – £60*

B562
More bedroom furniture from Norman & Stacey's catalogue of c. 1910.
Top row. A suite in "satin walnut".
Price Range: *£30 – £40 the lot.*
Middle row, left. Solid fumed oak chest in an 18th century style.
Price Range: *£20 – £30*

Middle row, centre. A combination "satin walnut" washstand, 4ft. wide.
Price Range: *£10 – £20*
Middle row, right. A Sheraton style cheval glass in mahogany with boxwood inlay.
Price Range: *£25 – £45*
Bottom row. A selection of shaving tables.
Price Ranges: *left: £20 – £30. The base is useable on other pieces*
                i.e. 18th century tripods.
                left centre: £10 – £20
                centre: £5 – £15
                right centre and right: £5 – £15

TP580

A good quality mahogany tea-poy of 1835-40 with a turned and fluted column on a flat platform base. The scrolled feet are raised on "gadrooned" circular buns echoed in the base of the column. Note the figuring of the mahogany used for the convex top and its lid. The two glass bowls from the interior are missing but the lids for the tea compartments remain.

Price Range: £90 – £110

TP581

TP581

A page of tea-poy designs from T. King's *Modern Style of Cabinet Work* showing the essentially Regency basis of his designs. It is believed that the tea-poy ceased to be made after 1850s had come to a close. The interior of the higher quality pieces usually contains two rectangular compartments, lined with foil made of zinc or tin, and one or two circular compartments into which a glass bowl or bowls were fitted for sugar and for mixing the teas. Many were made in rosewood but mahogany and walnut are also to be found, with walnut perhaps less common. Generally the glass bowls are missing and the foil lining has gone. If the interior has been gutted and the tea box lids are missing (or even the whole interior) then the value of the piece is considerably reduced.

Price Range: *£40 – £160. The wide range is due to the influence of high quality carving and the value points listed below.*

Value Points: *Carving *** The walnut example in TP671 illustrates the essential difference between this and simple examples such as TP583.*
Walnut ***
Yew ***
Rosewood **
Figured mahogany **
Complete interior (with original fittings) ****
Reasonably intact interior (with replacement glass bowls) ***

TP582

A mahogany tea-poy of c. 1840 with a hexagonal column in baluster shape supported on a flat base with turned feet. The latter have been carved with a petal form not unlike an elephant's toes. The top is rather more elegant, with a slimmer profile than the other examples and a reasonably intact interior. The glass bowl shown is, however, a replacement; it is very rare to find the original bowl inside or indeed the original silver fittings.

Price Range: £70 – £90

TP583

A plain mahogany tea-poy of c. 1840 with a flat platform base on turned feet. The centre column is plain turned and the only decoration to the top is the bead moulding around the edge of the lid.

Price Range: £50 – £70

TP584

A rosewood tea-poy of c. 1840 on a platform base with scrolled feet. The centre column is hexagonal although turned at the base. The concave sides were a popular design with this piece of furniture (see T. King's designs in TP580).

Price Range: £60 – £80

TP585

A walnut tea-poy ascribed to T.H. Filmer, Berners St., Oxford St., London c. 1845. The basically baluster shape of the centre column has been elaborated by the spiral twist turning and the top is veneered in burr walnut while the rest of the piece is made from the solid. The shape is unusual since most of the examples now available are rectangular.

Price Range: *£180 – £240*
Value Points: *Walnut ****

M590

A cheval dressing glass of c. 1820, precursor of many later Victorian models. Note the typical Regency features - the "bamboo" effect of the ring turning on the frame, the sabre-type legs ending in brass paw castors and the ebony stringing and inlay. In Victorian examples, the turning becomes heavier, with baluster forms, the sabre type legs are replaced by a flat platform or miniature cabriole legs and the mirror shape may become arched at the top.

Price Range: £90 – £120

M591

A typical mahogany dressing mirror of the mid-Victorian period, with the flat arch to the top which was prevalent from c. 1845 onwards. It might have been made much later, however, as Wyman's designs of 1877, overleaf, will confirm. Made in large quantities and not particularly scarce.

Price Range:	*£10 – £20*
Value Points:	*Condition of mirror ****
	Unusual woods **

M592

A page of dressing mirror designs from Wyman's *Cabinet Maker's Pattern Book* of 1877. Nearly always made in mahogany and with few distinguishing features between them save some carving of the uprights or a lidded compartment in the base.

Price Range: £10 – £20

M593

A walnut mirror on a circular marble-topped base, standing on a small mahogany chiffonier. The mirror is mounted in a typical support frame, refined by the outward curve and scroll at its ends. Note the carved and fretted decoration on the top of the mirror frame. c. 1850.

Price Range: *£20 – £30*

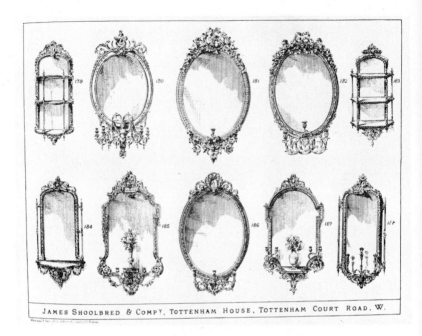

JAMES SHOOLBRED & COMPY, TOTTENHAM HOUSE, TOTTENHAM COURT ROAD, W.

M594

"Girandoles" from Shoolbred's catalogue of 1876. The decoration is made of plaster, subsequently treated with gesso and gilded. Until comparatively recently these ornate pieces were considered somewhat vulgar but prices have been mounting steadily in the last few years.

Price Range: £80 – £150

    (not to be confused with mirrors with frames of carved wood, whose prices are astronomical)

Value Points: *Condition of gilding ***. Re-gilding is an expensive job and frames which have been painted or gilt sprayed require complete restoration.*

    Condition of plasterwork ***. Ornate pieces which have missing or broken mouldings will also require expensive treatment.

M595

Glasses and girandoles from Shoolbred's 1876 catalogue. To economise on space the publisher has illustrated small girandoles inside the larger glasses but they are not part of them. The large glasses have a more limited market but have recovered from a position of undesirability some years ago to one of interest now. The small pieces have always had a good market.

Price Range: Large glasses   *£15 – £40 each*
                        Small glasses   *£30 – £50 each*
Value Points: *Condition of gilding and plasterwork ****

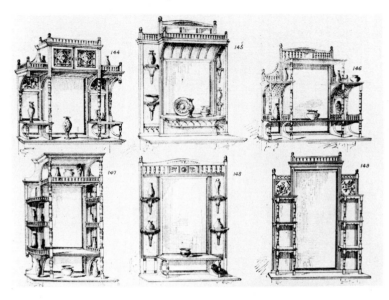

M596

Overmantels from Shoolbred's catalogue of 1876. Again the demand for these is comparatively recent and seems to come mainly from the European export trade. Certainly they are no longer smashed up and scrapped as in the past. They are of limited application, however.

Price Range: £15 – £30

SC610
Pole screens from T. King's *Modern Style of Cabinet Work* of 1829.
The pole screen is considered a decorative item but of limited functional
value. The use of embroidered and multi-coloured screen material provides the attraction; the stands themselves are often used as the basis
of a standard lamp conversion.
Price Range: *£20 – £35*

SC611

Three pole screens from Henry Wood's design book of c. 1850. The bases exhibit all the features of the period - scrollwork, finials, spiral twist turning etc. and these features are repeated in the frames of the screens. The material used for the screen would be Berlin woolwork and the floral effect would be highly decorative.

Price Range: *£25 – £45*

> *N.B. The pole screen allows the adjustment of the screen to the height required. They were used to screen the face from the fire or, if necessary, from direct light.*

SC612
Two cheval screens from Henry Wood's design book of c. 1850. These are clearly larger than the pole screens and would have been used to screen a fireplace, with or without a live fire in it. Again the constructional and decorative features of the frame are typical of the period.
Price Range: *£40 – £60*

SC613
A rosewood cheval fire screen of c. 1850, elaborately carved with scroll and leaf forms. The floral design is extremely decorative.
Price Range: *£35 – £60*

SC614

A walnut cheval fire screen of more "naturalistic" design c. 1850 with
an elaborate wool tapestry screen of heraldic design. The frame is carved
with leaf and floral forms. The cabriole type feet end in scrolls and the
whole effect is altogether simpler and freer than that of the previous
example, which retains a certain formality in the restraint of the turned
uprights but which has come only half way towards the freedom of this
one.

Price Range: *£60 – £90*

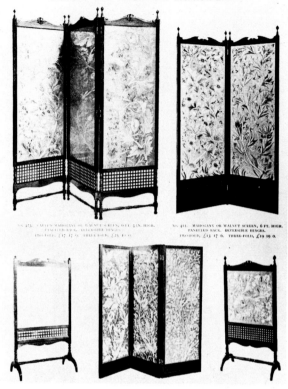

SC615

Screens from Norman and Stacey's catalogue of c. 1910. Note the essentially Edwardian features of the design, particularly the top right hand example, where the top frame exhibits the flattened broken pediment so often seen on the furniture of 1900-1910.

These folding screens are becoming popular, particularly those with decorative embroideries in good order. The cheval screens are not particularly sought after.

Price Range: *Folding screens   £40 – £80*
                      Cheval screens   £15 – £25
Value Points: *Brass and glass screens *****
                      Condition of embroidery ***
                      Oriental screens ****

V620

A Burmese chair. The experience and accumulation of Empire brought back quite a lot of Indian and Burmese furniture to Britain. This armchair and the cabinet overleaf are typical examples of Burmese furniture, still going round the shops in quantity. The taste for it has, perhaps understandably, died down. The amount of carving is astonishing but the effect somewhat overpowering; it is hard to incorporate into traditional decor.

Price Range: £40 – £70

V621

A Burmese cabinet-cum-chiffonier carved from teak or some other hardwood. The overall shape is similar to the normal designs of the period but the piece is so profusely carved that the effect is quite different. The craftsmanship is admissible but the taste is quite alien and one can understand the need to furnish a room completely in this manner rather than to combine it with European styles.

Price Range: *£80 – £150*

V622

A horrifying table with two candlesticks to match. It is not quite clear whether the 19th or the 20th century should be accused of producing it. The likelihood seems that it is about 70 or 80 years old. Awful. The wooden top is carved with obscure motifs and a souvenir name and date.

Price Range: *Unimaginable*

V623

An American invention, called the Wootton Patent Office Desk, of
about 1870 date. Doubtless it was extremely useful, especially for
executives of a magpie nature. There are several similar designs to be
seen in the auction rooms from time to time nowadays. They have not
so far attracted very high prices due to their lack of elegance and generally forbidding nature. Their turn may come however; like Wellington
or specimen chests they offer a means of concentrating more drawers
(and pigeon holes) per foot super than any other piece in the history
of furniture, except a bureau-bookcase.

Price Range: *£60 – £100*

V624

The subject of one of the ACC's 'Most Unfavourite Piece' series, this appalling mock-medieval, mock-Scandinavian bench probably takes the wooden spoon for fake oakery. There is no room to dilate here on its many failings as a fake (the ACC article does that) but it is worth recording that the Victorians love of the mediaeval was catered for by cabinet makers and joiners who, like those of the 1920s, 1930s and this decade, really meant not just to reproduce, but to deceive.

Price Range: *It was bought for £30 eight years ago, hopefully for real. As a garden bench it must be worth that, but sold within the last year for £65 – beauty is surely in the eye of the beholder!*

V625

A perfectly good oak bureau of the 18th century, utterly ruined by a Victorian "mediaevaliser". They did it to other pieces too - long case clocks have suffered particularly - and this form of carving was used very frequently. To those who don't know it, this bureau should not have any carving on it at all; it has all been added later. Oak, fruitwood and solid walnut bureaux have all been known to be vandalised in this fashion and then ebonised with a penetrating black stain to "age" them. Oak chests and coffers, genuinely of the 17th century, were often "improved" by adding this carving. It is almost as bad as the things they did to churches. The "restorers" solution nowadays is to plane down the carving and then veneer the piece in walnut; it has to be saw-cut veneer, though.

Price Range: *£50 – £100. Do not pay more; if you like it, you're a Philistine.*

V626

An Indian-made Davenport of extremely elaborate treatment. It is inlaid with ivory and other exotic woods and the gallery and columns are
considerably carved. The craftsmanship involved is enormous but the
overall effect slightly comical, particularly the elephant-like toenails
around the bun feet. A classic example of the genre.

Price Range: *Realised £410 at auction, June 1972.*

V627

A Bishop's throne-chair in oak. Gothic in style, with a canopy. The back is carved with formal flowers and an heraldic coat of arms with a coronet.

Price Range: *Auctioned for £220 in September, 1972.*

V628
A papier-mâché cabinet, decorated with mother of pearl inlay, gilt scroll work and painted scenes of castles in landscape settings. (Windsor Castle was a favourite subject.)
Price Range: *£350 – £500*

V629
A papier-mâché games table, again decorated with mother of pearl inlay, gilt scroll work and painted hunting scenes.
Price Range: £175 − £250

V630

A maple table with octagonal top on a "tripod" base of not uncommon design. The central orb and its bobbin-turned antennae are not unlike a small space satellite. Not suitable for heavy aspidistra pots. There are four real drawers and four "false" fronts under the top.

Price Range: *The week-end this photograph was taken, two examples were seen in the same Suffolk street, in shops, within 150 yards of each other. One was £35, the other was £12.*